TIFFANY TASTE

TIFFANY
TASTE

By John Loring

Doubleday & Company, Inc.

Garden City, New York
1986

Also by John Loring (with Henry B. Platt):
THE NEW TIFFANY TABLE SETTINGS

Color photographs preceding the title page are:
Dublin Weekend, see page 94
Sea Lion Lunch, see page 38
Lunch in the Rana Palace Garden, see page 64
Tiffany's Tea, see page 120
Fruits and Fruit Tisane, see page 156
Luncheon at Chanel, Inc., see page 176
FRONTISPIECE: Pasta Peretti, see page 66

Library of Congress Cataloging in Publication Data
Loring, John.
    Tiffany taste.

    1. Entertaining.   2. Dinners and dining.   3. Cookery.
4. Menus.   5. Table setting and decoration.   I. Title.
TX731.L58 1986   642'.4   85-29211
Copyright © 1986 by Tiffany & Co., Inc.
ISBN: 0-385-23584-4
All Rights Reserved
Printed in Japan
First Edition

Design by Jean-Claude Suarès
Assisted by Kathleen M. Gates

TIFFANY TASTE

Contents

Clippers and Caviar

I don't want a plane to leave without me," says Nancy Holmes, world-roving ambassadress for Pan American World Airways; and no one knows better the secrets of the good life aloft.

A longtime contributing editor of *Town & Country* magazine, she, through her research on stylish living from Aspen to Brunei, makes the first-class cabin of a Pan Am 747 a Holmes home. Here, on a Pan Am inaugural flight, she serves friends her favorite menu of lots of fresh black caviar.

Guests eat from Tiffany's yellow and blue "Monet" porcelain designed by Claude Monet for use in his garden house at Giverny. The crystal is Tiffany's exclusive Baccarat pattern, "Nemours." "Hamilton" flat silver and Portuguese floriform candlesticks complete the in-flight evening setting.

The caviar is served with a fork and fresh breadsticks, buttered at one end with a lemon-flavored butter, then rolled in finely chopped parsley. Other caviar dishes in the "good Holmes cooking" repertoire include two salads, one a Northern Italian classic of cold pinto beans, chopped onion, and Italian parsley, the other, a Scandinavian combination of diced cooked beetroots, red potatoes, raw scallions, and a few caraway seeds. Both are mixed with a light vinaigrette served on a bed of Boston lettuce and topped with a generous spoonful of sour cream and more fresh caviar. All are served in-flight with ice-cold brut champagne.

The "Nemours" water goblets in Mrs. Holmes's setting are strictly for ice and vodka.

Nancy Holmes

All Laborde

The ranches and cotton farms of southeastern Texas played a key role and knew enormous prosperity during the Civil War. By the post Civil War period, the area had grown rich, and in the thriving river towns along the Rio Grande, luxurious hotels were built to cater to pleasure-loving riverboat travelers, cattle barons coming to town to sell their herds, and military officers of the American Army's forts along the Mexican border.

In the 1890s Rio Grande City, some forty miles up the river from Port Isabel, in Starr County, Texas, was a hub of activities that were not without their own boisterous glamour. There on East Main Street, Françoise de Laborde built herself a fine verandaed red-brick house and travelers' way station in 1898 and '99.

Special pink-red bricks were made in Camargo, Mexico. Handsomely proportioned nine-over-six-pane double-hung windows with louvered interior shutters, elaborate "gingerbread" trim, and stair balusters were fashioned by European craftsmen then living in the Rio Grande region. The best wallpapers, Oriental rugs, and English Axminster carpets were bought to decorate the interiors; cast-iron gates, railings, and a fountain were imported.

As years passed and irrigation waters were pumped out, the Rio Grande changed its course. Riverboats became history and nearby Fort Ringgold lost its importance.

The officers and ladies who once frequented the Laborde vanished, and gradually the society that supported the sumptuous life-style of the house evaporated with the waters of the river.

Until a few years ago the once elegant hotel was little more than a ruin. Its present owners, Mr. and Mrs. J. Laurence Sheerin of San Antonio, decided to restore it to its turn-of-the-century magnificence.

Mrs. J. Laurence Sheerin

Through their good efforts the hotel, now on the National Register for Historical Places, has recaptured its past.

Mrs. Sheerin makes the entrance court the scene for a late Sunday lunch with a setting using Mason's "Tiffany Yellow Flowers." The English ironstone echoes the Texas sunflowers while old-fashioned red roses are grouped in shell-shaped Victorian silver "spoonwarmers." The flat silver is Tiffany's "Olympian," first introduced in 1878. There are Mexican silver service plates and engraved Mexican glass beer goblets from the crystal factories in nearby Monterey.

For lunch Mrs. Sheerin serves fresh asparagus with a hot hollandaise sauce loaded with capers, followed by a salad of Texas lettuce piled high with avocado, Gulf of Mexico shrimp, and Texas pink grapefruit dressed with a fresh dill vinaigrette. Mexican beer will be drunk throughout the meal, and a simple orange zest-scented crème caramel will be offered with coffee.

A bowl of fresh Texas vegetables and a pitcher filled with Texas scallions are a reminder of the produce that has once again brought prosperity to Starr County.

Each of the Laborde House's eleven "grand bedrooms" for guests has its own décor. Here in the Recámara Roja, visitors breakfast behind closed shutters on a variety of local Mexican sweet breads and fresh fruits from the neighboring ranches. Small hot wheat-flour tortillas filled with scrambled eggs, minced ham, and piquant green chili sauce will follow.

The Texas-Victorian breakfast table is set with Tiffany's "English King" flat silver. Dishes are in the Este "Grapevine" pattern. A Tiffany blue, Coalport porcelain perfume burner furnishes the table along with French porcelain jam and mustard pots bearing the monogram of the French King Louis-Philippe. The napkins, embroidered in Venice, bear the monogram of the Sheerins, and a Battersea "Rocking Horse" box holds vitamin pills.

Small hot wheat-flour tortillas filled with scrambled eggs, minced ham, and piquant green chili sauce

South of Laredo

In a Texas ranch house, Texans will be Texans, so Tiffany gold-and-enamel bracelets by Jean Schlumberger are used as napkin rings. Yellow roses bloom on the seventeenth-century Mexican table. Eighteenth-century Mexican silver altar reflectors shed candlelight and the great wines of France are poured into engraved Monterey Burgundy glasses.

The Tiffany silver is "Audubon" and the Tiffany Battersea enamel portrait box of Hollis, one of the family dogs, serves as a saltcellar.

Bowls of a fabulously rich red chili sauce will be used to dip a succession of fried and steamed fresh garden vegetables which are served as a first course. These will include Texas fifteen-percent-sugar corn, fried green tomato slices, steamed young okra, and "chiles rellenos."

The vegetables will be followed by Texas T-bone steaks grilled on a mesquite wood fire accompanied by roast sweet Texas onions.

The diners will sit on William and Mary gilt lacquer chairs in front of a two-hundred-year-old Mexican "Purgatory" cabinet.

Under the portico, beside the stately parade of stone columns carved in Guadalajara especially for the ranch house, an autumn lunch will be served on the rancher's fine collection of antique Mexican ceramics.

The candles held in Tiffany's exclusive Baccarat "Nemours" candlesticks flicker in the breeze that blows across the Bermuda grass lawn. Over two hundred imported palm trees offer a cool shade and give the ranch its name, Las Sombrillas.

Massed Texas sunflowers will oversee a lunch of barbecued kabobs of beef and pork tenderloin sprinkled with lime juice, served with a tomato and sweet onion salad. These will be

Tiffany & Co.

followed with slices of soft, ripe Gorgonzola cheese accompanied by fried, yellow cornmeal mush and sweet butter.

Plenty of cold white Spanish wine will be drunk out of Monterey water tumblers by guests while sitting regally in seventeenth-century Mexican armchairs.

Spanish brandy will be served with coffee before taking a tour of inspection in the ranch plane.

Texans will be Texans, so Tiffany gold-and-enamel bracelets by Jean Schlumberger are used as napkin rings

The House Befitting Heaven

The point of land at the northwest end of Waikiki Beach has for over a century been called Halekulani, which is variously interpreted in English as meaning the "house befitting heaven" or the "house befitting royalty."

The old frame beach dwellings of the wealthy that were clustered here at the turn of the century have long since been displaced by the Halekulani Hotel. And at today's Halekulani the view from the Presidential Suite, perched just above Waikiki Beach, is, as always, the sweetest in the world.

Here Princess Jean Liechtenstein, now a Honolulu resident, sets a small table to lunch quietly with the incomparable view of Diamond Head.

Tiffany's "Riviera" porcelain and "Century" flatware are used with a pair of late Ming vases and a rare K'ang-hsi peachwood brushpot for the Princess's flowers.

Lunch will be "shrimps Halekulani" sautéed with garlic and Pernod; grilled filet of mahimahi on spinach leaves with rosemary-citrus butter; then a glass of Halekulani iced tea with its flask of sugar syrup and possibly one of the hotel's traditional popovers served with delicious pale yellow poha jam.

Princess Jean Liechtenstein

Iolani Palace Dinner

n 1881, H.M. King David Kalakaua of the little island kingdom of Hawaii traveled around the world and thereby became the first reigning monarch to circumnavigate the globe. The royal retinue was composed of only three men, the king, a cabinet minister, and a manservant. They were fêted by Emperor Mutsuhito of Japan, Viceroy Li of China, the King of Siam, Pope Leo XIII, the Kings of Italy and Portugal, Queen Victoria and her son-in-law Crown Prince Friedrich of Germany, and finally U.S. President Chester A. Arthur.

Although Kalakaua's traveling companion, William Armstrong, wrote at the time that the little group "had much experience in dull table companions at royal banquets," and frequently longed for their island home, the Hawaiian king was dazzled by the grandiose trappings of more established royalty and determined to bring some reflection of them to his own court. To that end, he geared the completion of his new Iolani Palace to match, as best his finances would allow, his expanded vision of royalty.

By the time of his coronation on February 12, 1883, the Iolani was a curious triumph of Victorian eclecticism and comforts.

What Iolani lacked in size, it did not lack in festivity. "The Merry Monarch" made it the scene of elegant state dinners and balls; lavish entertainments with liveried palace servants, excellent food, and music by a band of native musicians presided over by "Mr. Berger," a German bandmaster sent to Hawaii by Kaiser Wilhelm I.

The band would break into Hawaiian songs such as "Akahi Hoi" or "Imi A Miau Oe" written by the music-loving king, or the lovely "Aloha Oe" written by his younger sister, Liliuokalani. But the tone was European, the men always in full dress or military uniform and

for King Kalakaua
and Queen Liliuokalani

the women in ball gowns from Worth of Paris.

If the king set the tone, evenings must have been merry indeed; for, as his drinking companion Robert Louis Stevenson wrote, "His Majesty is a fine intelligent fellow, but what a crop for the drink! He carries it like a mountain with a sparrow on its shoulder: a bottle of fizz is like a glass of sherry to him; he thinks nothing of 4 or 5 or 6 in an afternoon as a whet for dinner."

His dinners were no less daunting. A Wednesday night palace menu two days after the coronation lists four soups, eight fish, six entrées, seven roasts, one curry, nine vegetables, cheese, salad, six desserts, fruits, "pom-poms," seven wines, beer, liqueurs, tea and coffee.

The highly international foods, ranging from Windsor soup for the English, to boiled uhi, ulua, and oio for the Hawaiians, to boiled turkey with truffle sauce for the Americans and *à la mode* beef for the French, made up a menu of no great cultural depth but one that was undoubtedly satisfying.

The table settings at these great events included Baccarat crystal, French silver, and Puillivet procelain bearing the royal Hawaiian coat of arms given to Kamehameha IV in 1858 by Napoleon III, whose portrait hangs in the Iolani Palace dining room opposite the sovereign's throne-like dining chair.

One of the four soups was presumably served with the Tiffany "Olympian" silver soup ladle that belonged to Kalakaua's sister and successor, Liliuokalani, the last Hawaiian monarch and last occupant of the Iolani, America's only royal palace.

A Wednesday night palace menu . . . four soups, eight fish,
six entrées, seven roasts, one curry, nine vegetables, cheese,
salad, six desserts, fruits, "pom-poms," seven wines, beer,
liqueurs, tea and coffee

Tiffany Taste

Sea Lion Lunch, Regent Supper

he shabby, if madly picturesque, working junks of Victoria Harbour are akin only in name and basic structure to the languid pleasure boats found meandering about the channels and bays off the south shore of Hong Kong Island.

Here in Deep Water Bay, Regent International Hotels' impresario, Adrian Zecha, and his wife keep the *Sea Lion*, stylishly decorated for them by New York friend Pat Keller in natural varnished woods, faded denim, and copper.

The delightfully roomy deck of their junk is the scene of informal lunches while sailing across the East Lamma Channel to Picnic Bay or simply lolling at anchor at Deep Water.

The *Sea Lion*'s round wicker table is set with Tiffany's private stock "Carousel Chinois" china on place mats made of taro leaves. The silver is "Chrysanthemum." An antique black-and-gold lacquer box filled with exotic fruits from Hong Kong's markets decorates the table along with freesias in Tiffany's small Baccarat artichoke vases.

For lunch, paper-thin slices of beef "carpaccio" marinated in lemon juice and soy sauce will be grilled on charcoal braziers tended by the *Sea Lion*'s crew on the prow of the junk. These are served on a bed of lightly seasoned cold rice noodles and fresh bean sprouts and accompanied by a watercress salad and radish pickles.

The centerpiece of loquats, pungent and tantalizing durians, mangosteens, Japanese apples, star fruits, mandarin oranges, and grapefruit-like pomelos will complete the meal.

Back in the city, in a waterfront suite of their Regent Hotel, the Zechas dine quietly with a

Mr. and Mrs. Adrian Zecha

friend while enjoying the incomparable view from Kowloon across Victoria Harbour to neon-lit downtown Hong Kong.

Supper is served on Dorothy Hafner's "Tiffany Blue Dot" contemporary porcelain combined with the Regent's extravagant green jade table accessories. A seventeenth-century Ming brushpot holds chrysanthemums.

The light dinner focuses on specialties from the South China Sea, shark-fin soup followed by Mrs. Zecha's favorite "drunken shrimp" steamed in Chinese white wine. There will be a Regent specialty of sea scallops "larded" with bits of fresh firm pears and fried. And finally, Shanghai crabs steamed like their drunken cousins in Chinese white wine.

Languid pleasure boats found meandering about the channels and
bays off the south shore of Hong Kong Island

*Shanghai crabs steamed like their drunken
cousins in Chinese white wine*

Lunch in the New Territories

To create a propitious environment and live well, the Chinese say a person must have a finely tuned sense of "wind/water": competence at positioning things, be they buildings, plants, pools, or objects. A house should face south, with a mountain behind it, water before it, and protective hills to either side.

With the same sense of style which he brings to the selection of astonishing objects for his celebrated Hong Kong emporium, *Charlotte Horstman & Gerald Godfrey, Inc.*, Gerald Godfrey has exercised his sense of "wind/water" on a small jewel of a house and garden in the hills of the New Territories only moments from central Kowloon.

At the front of the house, which was built around 1920 in traditional South China style for the Anglican Bishop of Hong Kong, Mr. Godfrey has created a water garden of gravity-defying perfection.

A pool squared in deference to classical Chinese logic is broken and animated by a flat diagonal bridge of cadmium-orange lacquer. On either side of the bridge, the otherwise still waters erupt in bubbling and splashing fountains to the delight of the land-bound and the pool's many fish, those symbols of "marital bliss, prosperity, happiness, and everything good."

Northern Thai sculptures of storks and deer are souvenirs of Gerald Godfrey's sojourn in the Golden Triangle on the banks of the Mekong River, between Laos and Thailand. There, barking deer would come out of the tropical forest each evening to drink from the river. "Those deer," says Godfrey, "which are symbols of longevity and sweetness, were the most hauntingly beautiful sight."

The gardens are the settings of frequent meals with friends. The Godfreys offer not only all the products of the little farm that borders the gardens but also prime beef, veal, and lamb

Mr. and Mrs. Gerald Godfrey

brought from England, salmon from Scotland, and abalones from Tokyo.

On those humid Hong Kong days when air and water seem one, the Godfreys might lunch from a tray on their lacquered bridge. A faintly curry-flavored cream of pumpkin soup, cold salmon, and a salad made with a mixture of the organic herbs and vegetables from the garden might be served as they discuss some jewels and gemstones brought by one of Hong Kong's countless gem dealers. The silver is Tiffany's "Padova," designed by Elsa Peretti. The "Arabia" plates are from Tiffany's Private Stock collection.

At the end of the garden, a late-eighteenth-century Thai Buddha surrounded by orchids oversees the Godfreys' breakfast. After her husband's departure for their Ocean Center store, Cecily Godfrey may sit with one of the Peking guard beasts on the front step while finishing her coffee.

A house should face south, with a mountain behind it,
water before it, and protective hills to either side

Kathmandu Days

Ntil a little over thirty years ago, the tiny mountain kingdom of Nepal was off-limits to all foreigners. This policy of isolationism, coupled with the superb natural defenses created by the Himalayas to the north and the malaria- and tiger-infested swampy jungles to the south, made Nepal one of the most conservative and best preserved of civilized countries.

Lacking the West's modern amenities of dry-wall construction, local builders persist in their own form of "dry-wall" art. Using their innate genius as builders, they literally stack three- and even four-story houses out of meticulously formed and polished terra-cotta brick. Since Nepalese law still wisely forbids the exportation of all antiquities from the kingdom, balconies and roof timbers dating as far back as the thirteenth century are available for recycling.

The most passionately dedicated of preservationists in Nepal is Mr. Dwarika Shrestha. His enchanting museum/hotel, Kathmandu Village, houses the country's most remarkable collection of carved architectural elements.

Here, under the watchful care of the hotel's Swiss manager, Annemarie Spahr, guests learn the secrets of not only Nepalese art and architecture but also Nepalese cooking, at tables set in the dappled shade of fruit-laden persimmon trees. The lore of Nepalese food is rife with taboos of religion, superstition, and caste. This has produced a satisfying, sustaining, and healthy cuisine, which is prepared by Ms. Spahr's cooks with great dexterity, if not always complete orthodoxy.

Seated on dining chairs designed by Mr. Shrestha with back splats carved in the form of Nepalese "khona" swords, guests will lunch on traditional spinach and chicken. The chicken is sautéed in butter and oil, flavored with garlic, coriander, cloves, and black pepper and served

Dwarika Shrestha

on a bed of lightly sautéed spinach and tomatoes sprinkled with sesame seeds. Side dishes of rice and a sweet cucumber "achar" or chutney accompany the main course. The chutney is made with cucumber which is peeled, seeded, and diced, panfried in mustard oil, or "ghiu," and seasoned with fenugreek, chili powder, sesame seeds, and turmeric. The chutney is moistened with lemon juice, salted, and cooled.

Hindu superstition holds that root vegetables are "tamastic," begetting anger, envy, dullness, because they grow in darkness. But defiantly, the host serves carrots, made into a soupy cold pudding to be served in bowls with the chicken. This typical Nepalese dish, "cajarko kheer," is made by frying carrots in "ghiu" until softened, then boiling in sweetened milk. After this they are puréed, cooled, and garnished with a choice of stewed dried fruits.

A cold salted yogurt drink made from half yogurt and half water, lightly salted and flavored with crushed, fried cumin seed, will be served in bronze beakers; a surprisingly refreshing accompaniment.

The table setting has coordinated Ms. Spahr's favorite pink roses with Indian chintz napkins and Tiffany Private Stock "Rose Plaid" plates. The silver is "Audubon." An intricately carved bronze "tanpa" waterpot enriches the setting.

Just off the second-story stair landing of each Nepalese house a fancifully carved balcony affords Nepalese ladies a privileged spot for chatting, snacking, enjoying the afternoon breeze, and watching the world pass by. No ornamental detailing is too complex for these aeries, and no delicacies too rare to be savored within their confines.

On the balcony of the main house at Dwarika's Village, a tea is offered. The staccato black-and-white patterns of Tiffany potteries designed by Beth Forer play against the gentle interlacings of the lattices.

Tables set in the dappled shade of fruit-laden persimmon trees

Taking advantage of the plentiful persimmon trees that grow throughout the Kathmandu Valley, our host is serving a frozen egg custard with a sauce of persimmon pulp, sweetened with sugar syrup and dished out with an "Audubon" silver spoon.

Iced water, drunk from bronze or silvered beakers, is poured from a "karua," a spouted amphora, held by its own downturned rim.

The karua and beaker here come from nearby Baktapur, the capital city of a tiny kingdom of otherworldly beauty and charm, now a part of the kingdom of Nepal.

In a silvered beaker: "watermelon sherbat,"
a refreshing local drink, really a "squash," is made by
blending ripe watermelon pulp with a bit of milk or
yogurt and sugar to taste

Tiger Tops Tables

There are two ways to reach Nepal's Royal Chitwan National Park and Tiger Tops Jungle Lodge; both pass by the grassy Maghauly airfield on the banks of the Rapti River.

The seventy-five-mile plane trip from Kathmandu offers an hour's unparalleled view of the Himalayas. The mountain roads offer five hours of delightful insights into the colorfully picturesque life and breathtaking scenery of Nepal. The traveler slows his pace to fifteen miles an hour as he observes typical Nepalese sights, such as sleeping sacred cows, washed-out bridges, and village festivals.

After a few minutes' walk from Maghauly, native Tharu boatmen pole travelers across the crocodile-filled water of the Rapti. On the south bank, elephants wait to carry them through foot-deep mud and elephant-eye-high grass — the last lap of the journey to Tiger Tops.

The lodge sits in the middle of Chitwan's three hundred and sixty square miles of grasslands and jungles, once the private hunting preserve of Rana princes who as "prime ministers" ruled Nepal until quite recent times.

Setting out on a veritable army of elephants, the Ranas and their internationally titled guests hunted the plentiful Royal Bengal tigers, leopards, and great Indian one-horned rhinoceroses that made their home in Chitwan. No longer hunted, some three hundred rhinos and forty tigers go peacefully about their business today, enjoying the full support of His Majesty's Government in Nepal and the World Wildlife Fund.

Arriving at Tiger Tops, the guest is greeted by the lodge's director, Lisa Van Gruisen. It is early evening and the traveler has the chance to watch one of the greatest shows on earth, the sun setting on the Himalayas.

Lisa Van Gruisen

To better enjoy the spectacle, Mrs. Van Gruisen places her table for the evening meal at the edge of the jungle. From here she has a clear view across the feathery heads of a field of fifteen-foot elephant grass to the glorious panorama of the mountains. If weather permits, she will be able to see all the way from Annapurna Himal on her far left, across the Manaslu Group's 8,156-meter peak, to the clearly defined Ganesh Himal.

Her dinner will be eaten with "Audubon" silver from Tiffany's colorful handpainted Este ceramics, a bright contrast to the khakis, olive drabs, and beiges worn in the jungle to avoid agitating the animals.

The variety of fresh foods in jungles is limited, and a practiced hand with tinned ingredients is essential in maintaining civilized dining habits, as is a knowledge of cooking times to tame the jungle-grown vegetables.

Here Mrs. Van Gruisen sups on a cooked cucumber and tinned crabmeat salad topped with tinned prawns.

Cucumbers have been peeled, seeded, and salted, then thoroughly poached in white wine. Once chilled, they are mixed with lots of tinned lump crabmeat and fresh or bottled mayonnaise which is generously seasoned with black pepper, dill seed, a dash or two of Tabasco, and a bit of dry mustard. The salad is then covered with little pink tinned prawns or shrimp.

Although bread is generally not eaten with seafood dishes in Nepal, the crabmeat salad is accompanied by good Western-style home-baked bread and imported butter.

Fresh fruit sits on a "thal" dish woven of jungle leaves used on Nepalese feast days and a bronze "amkhora" contains decorative local grasses. The Este "Blue Bristol" plate holds decorative trompe l'oeil ceramic eggs.

Breaking the jungle's green-brown harmonies, the table is covered with a flamboyantly embroidered Kashmir shawl. The coffee and ices are served in Tiffany Private Stock "Jeu de Cartes" handpainted French porcelains.

Her breakfast is served by lantern light, as electricity is still unknown in the Chitwan jungle, and her table is set with Tiffany's "Red Vine" Coalport bone china and "Chrysanthemum" flat silver.

Sitting on the lodge's comfortably spacious, long-legged "elephant saddle" seats, the visitors enjoy coffee, a bracing cognac, and dishes of cooling lemon and peach milk ice. Sugar cookies filled with chopped peanuts are also served, and are a favorite of Tiger Tops' much spoiled baby elephant.

Lunch in the Rana Palace Garden

Ever since the Rana prime ministers turned Nepal back to the royal family, their many palaces have been "deconsecrated" and converted to modern use or simply let fall into ruin. A fleeting glimpse of the grandeur that once was Rana Kathmandu can be seen in the Yak & Yeti Hotel gardens where the regal white marble and ochre stucco palace now provides a handsome setting for banquets and other festivities.

Here, using the palace's three-tiered Palladian arched façade as a backdrop, Mrs. Stephen Halsey, English wife of the President of the American Express Foundation, sets a table to lunch with a Rana friend. The setting recalls the days when Victoria was Empress of India and the local prince reigned in splendor.

Two of the original palace ballroom chairs are drawn up to the table set with Tiffany "Fleurs sur Fond Gris" handpainted china. Their floral patterns are Europeanized descendants of the traditional flower motifs of the lacquered papier-mâché boxes imported from Kashmir. They are used here by Mrs. Halsey to hold Indian marigolds, pink roses, and blue Himalayan asters.

Kashmir bangle bracelets serve as napkin rings and a lacquered egg cup props up one perfect rose. The flat silver is Tiffany "Chrysanthemum" introduced in 1880 for just such settings.

A chilled fresh tomato soup flavored with fried cumin seeds and chopped chives is followed by a typical Nepali vegetable curry made from available mixed green vegetables. All are parboiled until tender but firm, then mixed with a pungent sauce made by blending fenugreek seeds and turmeric powder with crushed garlic, salt, finely chopped fresh ginger, chilies, and parsley, all fried in mustard oil. Nepali rice and "nam" bread accompany the curry.

The terra-cotta elephant planter behind the table evokes the days when Ranas set out from their palaces to hunt from elephant-back in the southern jungles of their country.

Mrs. Stephen S. Halsey

Pasta Peretti

assing through the old Roman wall at the top of the Via Veneto, the road arrives in a noble and inviting forest of umbrella pines. Then, a few steps, a few turns, a bell, an elevator, and doors open into the Roman rooftop kingdom of Elsa Peretti.

The legendary designer, as tall, as noble, and as inviting as the pines of Rome themselves, can often be found sitting with friends and favorite craftsmen on a terrace overlooking the Villa Medici, enjoying the sun and each other's company.

The tablewares will all be of her own sleek and personal design. There will be handblown plates and bowls of Venetian crystal, including her popular "Trattoria" plate. The silverware will, of course, be Elsa Peretti's "Padova" designed for Tiffany & Co. and named for the northern Italian city where it is produced.

In the evening, life chez Elsa assumes a more ordered tone in the airily grand, neo-classic dining room designed by Peretti's great friend, Renzo Mongiardino.

The tables are set with chrome yellow and French blue porcelains by another artist/designer, Claude Monet.

The sensually organic ceramic soup tureen is of unmistakable Peretti design as are the silver salt-and-peppers, the flat silver and glasswares.

Guests will be served from the voluminous tureen with a great Elsa Peretti favorite, "pasta e fagioli," the thick soul-warming Italian soup of beans and pasta cooked with chicken stock, a hint of thyme and rosemary, then generously topped with the best homemade olive oil.

The soup will be followed by a bowl of barely steamed spinach seasoned with olive oil and lemon juice and a roast shank of veal, whose Italian name, "stinco di vitello," provides amusement for the frequent foreign guests.

Elsa Peretti

Royal Visit to Kronberg

The twenty-sixth of April, 1895, was unseasonably cool and rainy. Queen Victoria of England had planned to spend part of her one-day visit to her eldest daughter's new home, Schloss Friedrichshof, inspecting the gardens and stables. But she was forced to stay indoors, venturing out only long enough to plant a tree beside the west façade.

The house, completed the year before on a 250-acre estate in Kronberg at the foot of the Taunus Mountains, was the home of the Empress Victoria of Germany, widow of Friedrich III and mother of Kaiser Wilhelm.

"Friedrichshof is a country house," said the empress, "and not a schloss according to German ideas; nothing to attract attention but everything to hold attention."

It has, however, everything to make life civilized and agreeable; and, despite the April showers, the two Victorias, mother and daughter, must have spent a happy day together.

They would have lunched under the small dining room's Victorian neo-gothic vaulted ceiling at a table for two, in front of the towering Renaissance Revival cabinet containing part of the Emperor Friedrich and Empress Victoria's collection of antique porcelains and faïences.

Their table is set with "Audubon" flat silver and Tiffany's "Victorian Red Plaid" porcelain. Half-standard tea roses from the Balmoral-inspired gardens laid out by the empress with

for Queen Victoria

her two English gardeners decorate the table. The roses' Chelsea "red anchor" jardinière is one of the many English objects in the house.

Lunch for the visit will begin with Queen Victoria's favorite Balmoral Castle soup, made from minced chicken meat and well-seasoned veal stock which is thickened with crumbled, hard-boiled egg yolks, bread crumbs, and heavy cream and garnished with chopped parsley.

The soup will be followed by a dish of panfried quail and wild mushrooms served on a bed of well-dressed salad with croutons and lardons. And, for a main dish, there will be another Balmoral favorite, Scotch callops.

The boneless cutlets or callops are thickly sliced from a cold loin roast of veal, rubbed with nutmeg, red pepper, and salt and fried in a generous amount of butter, then served in a sauce made from the pan butter, veal stock, mashed anchovy, a bit of grated lemon zest, dry mustard, finely chopped mushrooms, heavy cream, and a small glass of sherry.

In the kitchen, the callops are prepared to be served on Tiffany red and brown "Balmoral Plaid" plates. The sherry waits to go into the sauce in a mid-nineteenth-century green Bristol glass and decanter. The farm butter observed by a British lion from Vista Alegre sits on an English plate embossed with the crown and crest of the empress's brother, Edward, Prince of Wales.

The lunch will conclude with a baked lemon custard pudding and a compote of rhubarb.

Following lunch, the two Victorias will spend the afternoon in the library of Friedrichshof, where a fire has been built in the open Venetian-style fireplace carved, like the window mullions, of local Franconian sandstone.

A small table is set beside the Emperor Friedrich's open letter cabinet with a warming cognac and coffee in Tiffany "Jeu de Cartes" porcelain cups.

*"Nothing to attract attention but everything to
hold attention"*

The conversation, aside from remarks on a family wedding to take place the following day in Darmstadt, will be vigorously intellectual, following the bent of the empress, who was one of the most outspoken thinkers of the nineteenth century.

The talk will touch on the hostess's total disapproval of the militaristic policies of her son's "Iron Chancellor" Bismarck, and the empress may even risk her mother's disapproval by admitting her interest in the writings of Karl Marx.

Surrounded by her extensive personal and well-read library on the arts, literature, philosophy, and social studies, the empress will at later dates carry on similar conversations with her brother, Edward VII, her nephew, George V, and Queen Mary, and her less-fortunate nephew, Tsar Nicholas II, who shared none of her enthusiasm for the writings of Marx.

Dinner at Friedrichshof will be served at a formal table set in the Blue Saloon, whose eighteenth-century marble fireplace and graceful Louis XVI woodwork were saved by the empress from the demolition of the Russische Hof in nearby Frankfurt.

The table is set with Tiffany Private Stock "Fleurs sur Fond Gris" handpainted porcelain and "Chrysanthemum" silver.

In the center of the table "Rock Cut" crystal candlesticks stand beside a Reidel "Georgian Shell" bowl filled with fuchsias and other red and deep-pink garden flowers.

The mantelpiece's elaborate urn is Fürstenberg. The Sir Thomas Lawrence portrait supervising the scene is of an unknown English lady.

Dinner will not be a Dickens-style Victorian debauch of a "jolly round of beef" and "a ham of the first magnitude and sundry towers of buttered Yorkshire cake piled slice on slice in the most alluring order," but it will lack none of the generosity and variety of Victorian meals.

The generosity and variety of Victorian meals

There will be cream of fresh white asparagus soup followed by a course of fresh trout dipped in beaten egg and Irish oatmeal and fried in butter.

This will be followed by a second course of a very German roast saddle of venison with green pepper corns served with wild cranberries and chestnut purée and a very English boiled "corned" leg of lamb with caper sauce.

The lamb will have been soaked in a brine of water, salt, sugar, bay, and pepper for two days before boiling in fresh water.

The caper sauce will be made with a rich "roux": chicken stock, capers, and lemon juice thickened with egg yolk.

There will be a third course of roast guinea fowl and lobster salad followed, or "removed," by a gooseberry tart with plenty of vanilla-flavored "schlag."

Before retiring, the empress will sit quietly and have coffee by the fireplace in the sitting room of her private apartment. Her chair, whose cushion is embroidered with her imperial arms, sits beneath a portrait of her brother, the Prince of Wales. Bronze busts of herself and her husband, Friedrich III, in younger days, sit on the mantelpiece. A revealing and penetrating portrait of her mother, Queen Victoria, painted in 1875 by Heinrich von Angeli hangs across the room, and family photos share the fireside table with a Fürstenberg porcelain coffee set.

Along with coffee an "Empress Pudding," once a favorite of Prince Albert, will be offered as a "snack." The rice pudding, rich with eggs and butter, the top half flavored with currant jelly, the bottom half flavored with peach jam, is decorated with candied ginger and more currant jam. It is served with a hot brandy-flavored custard sauce.

The Empress Victoria's Friedrichshof, which exists today as Schlosshotel Kronberg at Kronberg in Taunus, retains in its atmosphere and cuisine all the excellence, beauty, and charm of the long-ago day of Queen Victoria's visit.

Queen Victoria's favorite Balmoral Castle soup, made from minced chicken meat and well-seasoned veal stock, which is thickened with hard-boiled egg yolks, bread crumbs, and heavy cream

Before retiring, the empress will sit quietly and have coffee by the fireplace in the sitting room of her private apartment. Her chair, whose cushion is embroidered with her imperial arms, sits beneath a portrait of her brother, the Prince of Wales. Bronze busts of herself and her husband, Friedrich III, in younger days, sit on the mantelpiece. A revealing and penetrating portrait of her mother, Queen Victoria, painted in 1875 by Heinrich von Angeli hangs across the room, and family photos share the fireside table with a Fürstenberg porcelain coffee set.

Dinner with Louis XV

In the midst of the unusually severe winter of 1748, the thirty-eight-year-old French king, Louis XV, paid an official visit to his beautiful young mistress, Madame de Pompadour. The scene of their meeting, the newly constructed palatial Château de Bellevue, was one of the Pompadour's many gifts from Louis.

As he entered, she received him in an immense greenhouse banked with every imaginable spring flower: roses, lilies, narcissi, dianthus, anemones, hyacinths, and tulips. Louis, who was always pleased with Mme. de Pompadour's artifice, was at first glance delighted, then delight was followed by rapture, when he realized that this floral extravaganza was entirely artificial.

Mme. de Pompadour had wished to introduce her king to the products of the seven-year-old porcelain manufactory at Vincennes of which she, as his official "Protectrice of the Arts," was patron. The king was impressed to the point of ordering on the spot some eight hundred thousand livres of Vincennes flowers in porcelain vases for his country houses.

A few months later, in the early spring of 1749, the confident and willful Mme. de Pompadour put Vincennes porcelain flowers on public sale and announced to the court that "no one is a true citizen of France who doesn't buy as much of this porcelain as money will allow." Mme. de Pompadour was a woman who meant business, and she got the court's business. Porcelain never bloomed so prolifically in France, or any other place, for that matter.

The Marquise de Pompadour took seriously her role as "Protectrice of the Arts." From the day in 1745 when she became Louis XV's official mistress, she became an inspired directress and propagandist for Vincennes. She called on the king's goldsmith, Duplessis, to design new forms, and on the best flower and chinoiserie painters of the day to invent new decorations.

for Mme. de Pompadour

To brighten the wildly mannered rococo designs she always preferred, she demanded new colors. "Bleu céleste" was created for her in 1753, followed by a rich pale green a year or so later. In 1758, the color most associated with her, "rose Pompadour," was first used at Sèvres.

If Louis XV and the Pompadour were to dine together today off Vincennes porcelains of "bleu céleste," their table would be set with Tiffany's "Blue Wave" china remade in conjunction with the Musée des Arts Décoratifs in Paris from a prototype in the museum's collections. Their silverware would be "English King." They would dine on fresh foie gras from the Pompadour's native Limousin, sautéed with fried apples and served with a salad dressed with walnut oil. There would be tiny spring lamb chops and grilled cèpes, and for dessert a heart-shaped "tarte Tatin." The caramelized apple upside-down cake would be served with crème chantilly decorated with candied violets and "Pompadour pink" rose petals.

During dinner the marquise would offer the king a lesson in design, commerce, and the seductive power of beauty, both natural and artificial.

The caramelized apple upside-down cake would be served with crème chantilly decorated with candied violets and "Pompadour pink" rose petals

Dinner with Louis XVI

Chinoiseries had been wildly popular in France since 1670 when Louis XIV built the Trianon de Porcelaine in the park of Versailles as a dining pavilion for himself and Madame de Montespan, and they persisted right up and into the French Revolution.

As late as 1792, only moments before the internment of the royal family in the Conciergerie on August 10 of that year, the Royal Porcelain Manufactory at Sèvres was producing an extensive service decorated with a circle of finely painted gold and platinum Chinese pastoral scenes on a black background.

The Sèvres porcelains lack the boldness of the earlier chinoiseries of Louis XV's time; the Chinese and their fretwork pavilions have all retreated to the outer rims of the plates. But they convey the finesse and grace that typified the court of the young Louis XVI and Marie Antoinette.

How poignant to imagine the king and queen, in their last days of semi-freedom, dining in the mob-encircled Tuileries off this intriguing dinner service.

Nostalgia for the extravagant picnics at "le Hameau," the faux-farm Louis had built for her at Versailles, and the frugality of mid-revolutionary life dictate a dinner of simple eastern French peasant foods: roast duck with braised sauerkraut, and potatoes sautéed with onions, bacon, and garlic.

The royal table stands beside a superb Louis XV "chinoiserie" secretary whose black-and-gold Japanese lacquer panels echo the black-and-gold Tiffany Private Stock "Nuits de Chine" porcelains. Square-based silver candlesticks maintain a sober republican air. The Japanese Revival flat silver is "Audubon," named for the great French-American naturalist-painter who

for Marie Antoinette

*A dinner of simple eastern French peasant foods: roast duck
with braised sauerkraut, and potatoes sautéed
with onions, bacon, and garlic.*

was once thought to be the royal couple's lost son Charles, known as "Louis XVII."

In the kitchen a "Nuits de Chine" tureen whose lines are already neo-classic holds the fresh sauerkraut braised with carrots, onions, butter, and Alsatian white wine, then covered with quarters of liberally salted and peppered roast duck.

The glass mustard pot is antique Louis XVI French glass.

The cook's "coupe de vin blanc" is in a paneled Austrian crystal glass engraved with hearts and lovebirds in Tyrolean folk art style. It is copied from glasses used at the festivities in Vienna on February 12, 1736, celebrating the wedding of Marie Antoinette's mother, Maria Theresa, Archduchess of Austria and Queen of Hungary and Bohemia, to Francis of Lorraine, Grand Duke of Tuscany.

The roast duck will evoke memories of Marie Antoinette's childhood at Schloss Schönbrunn before her wedding at the age of fifteen to the Dauphin, Louis. The sobering circumstances of 1792 will promote speculation on the couple's hopes of a foreign invasion from the east, and deliverance by the queen's nephew, the new Austrian emperor, Francis II.

As there is no bread available at the Tuileries, the queen has suggested to the kitchen staff "qu'ils mangent de la brioche!" so, in the fashion of Brittany, a cold chocolate mousse will be served for dessert accompanied by slices of a large sweet brioche.

The Sèvres porcelains lack the boldness of the earlier chinoiseries of Louis XV's time; the Chinese and their fretwork pavilions have all retreated to the outer rims of the plates. But they convey the finesse and grace that typified the court of the young Louis XVI and Marie Antoinette. How poignant to imagine the king and queen, in their last days of semi-freedom, dining in the mob-encircled Tuileries off this intriguing dinner service

A Modest Proposal
for Dinner

he great dining room of the Deanery of St. Patrick's Cathedral in Dublin is now the scene of family meals of the Very Reverend Victor Griffin, his wife, and their twin sons, but the room is still imbued with the spirit of Dean Griffin's eighteenth-century predecessor, Jonathan Swift, that complex, compelling, and most personal of authors.

As the "state portrait" of Swift by the Irish Palladian architect and painter Francis Bindon looks down from its Grinling Gibbons style frame, it is easy to imagine the great Dean of St. Patrick's, a man whose playful insults and friendly vituperations probably caused him to dine alone on more than one occasion, eating in solitary splendor at the head of his table.

As we picture the author of *Gulliver's Travels*, *A Tale of a Tub*, and *The Battle of the Books*, let us imagine him in 1729. In this, his sixteenth year as dean, he muses on the shocking course of action he is about to outline to Ireland's absentee English landlords in *A Modest Proposal*, that triumph of wit and humanity that remains to our day the greatest short satire in English literature.

Could the stuffed roast chickens suggest the roast Irish infants Dr. Swift is about to mockingly propose to the English?

In any case, the author of Gulliver's dinner does not propose the "mash of oats and milk," that "insipid diet" of the temperate and dull Houyhnhnms. Nor does his repast resemble Gulliver's barely more appealing toasted oatcakes and milk, accompanied by boiled herbs and a roast bird

for Jonathan Swift

or rabbit, all "at a great loss for salt." No, here is an intemperate feast, food fit for the emperors of Lilliput and Blefuscu.

Just as Jonathan Swift's wonderful writings are stuffed with the colors and substance of human thought, his chickens are stuffed with spicy sausage meat, rice, pignon nuts, chopped celery, and a bit of onion and dried currants imported from "Lilliput." There are boiled Irish potatoes, still quite new to Ireland in Swift's time, served in an Irish silver "potato ring" and a fresh, dark, moist Irish soda bread hot from the brick oven.

There is a dish of the salt that Swift claimed "was first introduced only as a provocative to drink," and drink there will be in abundance, for, as he said of his Ireland, "there is no nation yet known, in either hemisphere, where the people of all conditions are more in want of some cordial to keep up their spirits than ours."

The robust red Burgundy will be imported from "Blefuscu," as is still the habit in England and Ireland. The wines are served in Simon Pearce glasses.

The roast chickens will be followed by a plate of cold cooked salads, boiled sea kale, grilled endives, and braised lettuce served with soft cheeses. The meal is followed by Dean Swift's favorite nightcap of "bishop," which is simply a hot toddy of port flavored with roasted clove-stuck orange, cinnamon, mace, fresh ginger, lemon peel, sugar, and water.

From a Wedgwood-blue niche at the side of the dining room a bust of the good dean looks on. A bunch of ornamental Irish thistles sit at the base of Swift's statue, presumably dropped there from the fetlock of a friendly Houyhnhnm.

His chickens are stuffed with spicy sausage meat, rice, pignon nuts, chopped celery, and a bit of onion and dried currants

Dublin Weekend

The great, the near great, and others hopelessly enchanted with Ireland will all tell that one of the world's unsurpassed delights is a weekend spent as the guest of Sybil Connolly, Ireland's congenial leading lady of fashion, design, charm, good old-fashioned hospitality, and other things cultural.

Whether examining new weaves and patterns for Sybil Connolly dresses and accessories, or comparing recently arrived color proofs of her designs for Brunschwig & Fils or Martex sheets, Miss Connolly's perceptions of all things agreeable in life make her not just good company, but the best company.

No guest who has stayed in the Georgian mews house at the far end of the Connolly garden will soon forget the breakfasts and suppers served in the airy little guest dining room decorated with its handsome collection of blue and white Irish delft.

Breakfasts here, if one is fortunate and has said the right things to James the butler, will include

Sybil Connolly

grilled Irish bangers and green figs picked from the tree just outside the window.

Suppers focus on the abundant seafood for which Dublin is celebrated. There may be succulent Wexford mussels steamed in a little white wine and served with an inordinate quantity of chopped shallots and parsley. This might be followed by "Dublin lawyer," a simple dish of lobster meat sautéed in butter, flambéed with Irish whiskey, and mixed with heavy cream. On warm summer evenings, there may be "poor man's lobster," a salad of cold poached cod and parsnips on a bed of greens topped with mayonnaise and capers, to precede a small turbot steamed over watercress. "The great dessert then," says the hostess, "is always coeur à la crème, and it's terribly important that it be made in a proper basket."

These simple "family" meals for friends are served on "Ostendia" blue-and-white china accented by antique blue-and-yellow Chinese bowls and bits of the house's blue-and-yellow Tiffany Private Stock "Bigouden" porcelain.

Afternoons at Sybil Connolly's are often spent strolling about the garden. One notes the fine markings of a favorite dianthus and the green-petaled faces of the perennial border's rare clump of Irish Molly, soon to be used in a new design. Tea is served with a still-warm currant cake and small sandwiches made from the peppery nasturtiums that grow just beyond the terrace. A paper plate painted with a new pattern for Tiffany china could be brought on the tea tray, to see how well it works in the afternoon's rituals.

One evening of every weekend there is a formal dinner in the dining room of the main house overlooking Merrion Square. Without fail there will be a first course of little Norway lobsters called Dublin prawns served all plump and pink, nestled in the center of a cool pale green ring of avocado mousse. The meal will end with Sybil Connolly's rum-flavored chocolate mousse.

Such luxuries call for a table setting of Tiffany Private Stock "Fleurs sur Fond Gris" china, vermeiled silver beakers, eighteenth-century Chelsea porcelain-handled cutlery and, of course, little silver-gilt Dublin prawns cavorting about an oversized cabbage soup tureen.

Green figs picked from the tree just outside the window

*One evening of every weekend there is a
formal dinner in the dining room of the main house
overlooking Merrion Square*

*Tea is served with a still-warm currant cake and small
sandwiches made from the peppery nasturtiums that grow
just beyond the terrace*

In an Irish City Garden

Those high up in horticultural circles term it "one of the great gardens of our time": the enchanted acre of some three thousand varieties of plants and grasses, vines and flowers belonging to the Valentine Dillons in central Dublin. The Honorable Mrs. Dillon, whose one-woman masterpiece this is, is not an enthusiastic gardener; rather, she is a passionate orchestrator of nature's subtly nuanced forms, colorings, and textures.

When not actively gardening or helping run the family antique business, the Dillons enjoy late summer evening meals on the garden's center allée lawn in earshot of the gentle splashings of their dizzily Victorian cast-iron fountain. This, like the Irish Victorian cast-iron garden furniture, came to them straight from Dillon Antiques.

Their dinner is served on Tiffany Private Stock "Red Vine" china. The light claret is in antique Georgian Irish crystal goblets and a Victorian Staffordshire majolica acorn vase holds agapanthus, clematis, bellflowers, and false indigo selected from the vast variety of blue flowers that ornament the house. A "Tiffany Blue" English china mouse appears to be enjoying crumbs from the traditional Irish soda bread.

The dinner begins with a cool Irish summer soup of a thick, rich chicken stock flavored with mixed spring herbs and apples and garnished with mint. This will be followed by cold poached Irish salmon left in a mild pickle for twenty-four hours before serving and accompanied by chilled parboiled cauliflower pickles flavored with bay leaf, nutmeg, and clove. There will also be two vegetable dishes, delicately orange-flavored carrot flan and a purée of cooked watercress, potatoes, chopped parsley, and sour cream.

A dessert follows of fresh blackberries and raspberries mixed with ripe melon balls, chopped mint leaves, and sugar, served with small cinnamon-and-lemon-peel-flavored oatmeal cakes.

The Honorable Mrs. Valentine Dillon

Slane in the Sixties

Slane Castle sits on an eminence overlooking the River Boyne on the site of an earlier fortress in County Meath, not far from the Battlefield of the Boyne. Built in the 1780s by James Wyatt in Gothic Revival style, Slane Castle is the seat of the Conynghams. Although the family's ancient and cryptic motto, "Over Fork Over," probably has little to do with table etiquette, the feasts and fantasies of the table are much a part of Slane's past and present.

It was at Slane that the recently crowned and recently widowed King George IV arrived on the afternoon of August 24, 1821, to spend some days being entertained by his beautiful paramour Elizabeth, 1st Marchioness of Conyngham. The entertainments met with success and the marchioness remained George IV's favorite until his death nine years later.

The bon vivant English king left reminders of his stay at Slane in the form of three gilt-bronze statues, one of Frederick, Duke of York, and two of himself, the first standing in a toga

The Earl of Mount Charles

and the second dressed as a Roman general astride a prancing horse. The statue of the king as a Roman general is a reminder of his arrival at Slane on that August afternoon when George had ridden on alone ahead of his household suite and cavalry escort, covering the road from Dublin to Slane in exactly three hours. This feat greatly impressed not only the Marchioness Elizabeth but also the thousands of loudly cheering and loyal peasants who lined the roads to see him pass.

The three statues remained in the dining room of the castle until its current owner, Henry, the Earl of Mount Charles and son of the 7th Marquess of Conyngham, brought them to ornament his East Sixties apartment.

In their new setting of no less grand proportion, they look totally at home. George and his mount now sit proudly atop the salon's original marble New York townhouse fireplace, flanked by Tiffany neo-classic urns filled with cosmos, lilies, and tuberoses. Dinner guests are seated on Louis XVI chairs originally from the Slane drawing room and are entertained at a dinner table set with Tiffany Private Stock "Framboise Blanche" porcelain, vermeil "Hampton" flat silver, "Tiffany Swag" crystal, and a Venetian crystal "sweetmeat tree" centerpiece.

The food, like the table linens, will be Irish. Irish smoked salmon is served with fresh green figs. Roast lamb is basted with sweet cider spiced with a bit of clove, ginger, and lemon and served with a purée of turnips, carrots, and yams. A salad is made from the two ingredients most basic to Irish food — potatoes and cabbage — and is dressed with sour cream combined with chopped hard-boiled eggs, dry mustard, lemon juice, white vinegar, sugar, salt and pepper.

In honor of the 1st Marquess of Conyngham whom George IV made constable of Windsor Castle and steward of the household, "Poor Knights of Windsor" will be offered at dessert. "Poor Knights" is a Victorian favorite made of strips of sherry-flavored french toast topped with sugared berries and whipped cream.

A salad of potatoes and cabbage dressed with sour cream
combined with chopped hardboiled eggs, dry mustard, lemon
juice, white vinegar, sugar, salt and pepper

Tiffany Taste

Birr Castle Garden Lunch

uilt in the seventeenth century from remains of the medieval gatehouse of the Black Castle of the O'Carrolls, Birr Castle stands guard over St. Brendan's town of Birr on the banks of the River Camcor in County Offaly in the center of Ireland. The castle has housed fourteen successive generations of the Parsons family, who, for nine generations, have held the title of the Earldom of Rosse. Each generation has found it their great pleasure to continually improve the remarkable gardens and arboretums that cover Birr's famous park. The area is a small paradise comprising trees and flowers from every corner of the globe: Chinese wing nut, Andean barberry, Japanese bitter orange, blue Atlas cedar, and Monterey cypress.

At the far end of the formal gardens, past a towering box hedge that the Guinness Book of Records lists as the tallest in the world, are Birr's kitchen gardens. They provide the ingredients for the many seventeenth-century dishes that are still made at Birr from recipes preserved in a treasured family book in the castle. The *Book of Choyce Receipts* by Dorothy Parsons contains many of the Earl and Countess's favorite recipes, each written by hand and dating from 1686. No dish pleases the castle's current occupants more than one called "hartichoke pie." The globe artichokes that grow in prodigious quantity in the kitchen garden are direct descendants of the "hartichokes" Dorothy Parsons used in the seventeenth century and descendants of those brought from France in 1066 with the Norman Invasion of England.

On fine summer days when the Rosses find a quiet moment for a garden lunch, a table is set in the walled parterre garden beneath the imposing east tower, an original "flanker" of the Black Castle's gatehouse. The table service includes Tiffany Private Stock "Carousel Chinois" porcelain as well as antique, early Coalport flowered china, antique French and Spanish gilt

The Earl and Countess of Rosse

glasswares, and eighteenth-century Parsons family silver. A Victorian silver and crystal epergne overflows with ferns and flowers from the walled garden: old-fashioned roses, lavender, Nile lilies, cosmos, malvas, and flax.

In the basement kitchens, housed in the archways of the old O'Carroll castle gatehouse, lunch will be prepared from speckled trout caught by Lord Oxmantown, the Rosses' teenage son, and globe artichokes picked from the garden.

The food will be served from the castle's nineteenth-century Mason's ironstone "Nightingale" pattern platters and tureens.

The trout are to be simply barbecued over charcoal and dill stalks. "When they're just out of the river, they're nicer without sauce or things," observes the Countess of Rosse.

The artichokes will be boiled and the hearts layered in a baking dish with cooked pigeon or chicken meat and pieces of beef bone marrow that have been coated with egg yolk. The entirety is covered over with a custard of beaten egg and milk flavored with grated orange and lemon peel, ginger, nutmeg, cinnamon, salt and pepper and baked into a perfect "hartichoke" pie.

There will be raisin bread, soda bread, and white bread, all three baked in the castle twice weekly, and afterward, "Chrissy," the pastry cook, will have made ice cream and a marmalade tart with wonderful flaky pastry. "Not exactly mille-feuille, but it does go into layers," the countess observes.

Flowers from the walled garden: old-fashioned roses, lavender,
Nile lilies, cosmos, malvas, and phlox

Tiffany's Tea

The rocky, island-studded seacoasts of Devonshire, Warwick, Pembroke, and Southampton are not, despite their names, to be found around the British Isles but five hundred and eighty miles east of North Carolina on the island of Bermuda.

These parish names do honor less to Great Britain than to the memory of great money and eight London-based investors. These were the Bermuda Adventurers, who financed the "Somers Islands" colonization in the early seventeenth century and divided its nineteen square miles into eight "tribes."

In the intervening years, the English "tribal" system has undergone internationalization by Spanish and French colonials, pirates, Africans, Americans, and other seafaring peoples. They have produced a style yet to be defined but commonly denominated as "Bermudan."

This is the land of morning glories and marlins, onion fields and sailing races, of croquet lawns and cassava pie, planter's punches and swimming pools. It is the land of dignified colonial mansions by Robert Adams and pretty pink cottages with stepped white roofs by no one in particular.

On Sundays, the descendants of Caribbean farm boys and buccaneers breakfast on a traditional combination of salt codfish and boiled potatoes. The descendants of Anglo-Saxon and Norman nobility enjoy tea parties on their immaculate Bermuda grass lawns.

The local Sunday breakfast of cod and potatoes, reminiscent of a French "aioli," is served with fried plantains, raw avocado, and "turned cornmeal" and two sauces. One sauce is made of coarsely chopped cooked bacon, raw onion, fresh peeled tomato, and Italian parsley seasoned with olive oil and salt; the other is a loose, homemade mayonnaise loaded with finely chopped

Mrs. John A. Scrymgeour

hard-boiled eggs and raw green onion.

The more Anglican Sunday tea is served with a proper assortment of homemade breads and imported biscuits, tea sandwiches, candies, and an appropriately elaborate cake.

At the Scrymgeour home overlooking a point of the island where land, sky, and sea blend into each other, Mrs. John Scrymgeour sets a Sunday tea table.

The tables, dressed in a red geranium chintz organized by geranium red Chinese frets, are set with "Monet" blue-and-yellow porcelain repeating the festive colors of a nineteenth-century Chinese palace garden seat, also of porcelain, used at teatime as a side table. The "Shell and Thread" flat silver is Tiffany's, as is the silver tea service.

Small silver cups of yellow Bermuda lilies and pink oleanders ornament the table. On the porcelain garden seat a silver vase of yellow frangipani rests on books about the multitude of other flowers that cover Bermuda.

The hostess has set out a rival bouquet of silk flowers to brighten her tea party with their more sophisticated hues.

Along with the traditional hot tea there are water goblets filled with minted iced tea, more suited to summer afternoons on the islands.

The color coordinating cake is a "génoise" filled with fresh strawberries and a French "fraise-des-bois" white alcohol-flavored mousse.

This is the island of morning glories and marlins, onion fields
and sailing races

Callithea Croquet

Those versed in the intricacies of vacations in Greece will recognize Callithea as the name of a postcard-picturesque town on the island of Rhodes.

Those gifted at unraveling Greek island vernacular will know that to translate this name as "beautiful goddess" could be too scholarly. "Beautiful view," the French "Bellevue," would be more appropriate.

Those with knowledge of the Anglo-aristocratic sport of croquet could testify that Callithea is not Greek at all, but the Bellevue Avenue home of former Rhodes scholar Richard Pearman, the Young Presidents Organization International Chairman and international croquet champion.

Pearman's career began with a "blue" in golf at Oxford. His two championships in U.S. and Bermuda singles and three in Bermuda doubles have landed him in the Croquet Hall of Fame. He represented Bermuda five times in the Eisenhower Trophy, and he doesn't want it overlooked that he's "watched Wimbledon seventeen years in a row," or that rumor in the sporting world has it that "they put ditto marks on trophies for Dick Pearman."

The lawn at Callithea is familiar turf to croquet enthusiasts around the world. It also once served as a landing pad for the Air Force One helicopter carrying Richard Nixon. On special occasions, when not occupied by sports or helicopters, it could be the congenial setting for a Pearman family dinner.

Mrs. Pearman brings the colorful stylishness to her dinner tables that she more publicly displays at Triangles, her fashionable boutique in Hamilton.

At croquet lawn dinners there will be a crisply flowered tablecloth printed with little wild cyclamens and violets and punctuated by lushly tropical blossoms picked from the flowering hedges that surround the croquet lawn. Pink linen napkins will bloom from antique Art Deco

by Mrs. Richard S. L. Pearman

wine goblets enameled with processions of little infant Bacchuses. Chilled hock will be poured from Victorian cut crystal and silver-gilt carafes, and candles held by Tiffany "Rock Cut" candlesticks will flicker in tall hurricane chimneys.

The first course of a cold cream soup is served in pink ceramic rose bowls. The soup is made with finely chopped steamed shrimp, raw tomato filets, and mango mixed with thickened chicken stock and heavy cream and flavored with grated fresh ginger, saffron, and fresh Bermuda thyme.

This will be followed by a whole salmon trout steamed and served with mayonnaise spiked with a bit of Outerbridge's Bermuda Sherry Peppers Sauce. There will be creamed small onions and steamed new potatoes, both from the Pearman garden which produces all the vegetables for their table.

The meal will conclude with a salad of avocados filled with chopped tomato and Bermuda onion in a classic vinaigrette, followed by an open banana tart and lightly sweetened, rum-flavored whipped cream.

In case of a tropical shower, a painted tole Afghan hound umbrella stand guards golf umbrellas. "Vasco da Gama," the five Pearman children's Portuguese water dog, guards Mr. Pearman's croquet mallets carved from lignum vitae wood found in a three-hundred-year-old shipwreck off the Bermuda coast.

Vasco, a sports hound, is able to dive down ten to twelve feet into the water to catch fish which the children claim he then delivers to Doris the cook. Doris claims this is a myth.

Vasco ignores the rabbits gamboling on the lawn. They are made of Herend porcelain and pieced-together Ming shards and are not dedicated herbivores.

A crisply flowered tablecloth printed with little wild
cyclamens and violets and punctuated by lushly
tropical blossoms

*Chilled hock will be poured from Victorian cut crystal
and silver-gilt carafes, and candles will flicker in tall
hurricane chimneys*

Shipwrecked

hether the treacherous waters off Bermuda boast more shipwrecks than the gentle land boasts onions is open to dispute, and as the natives can guarantee, any island dispute is best settled over a long planter's punch.

The secret formula for this punch is open to social discussion. Old Bermudians, after admitting that the powdered spice on the punch's frothy top is to all evidence nutmeg, will go on and explain that "there are several kinds of fruit juice and a couple of rums, and an agent that holds the whole thing together. But the secret is held in trust, and the gentleman's obligation is to keep that trust. One thing certain, though, is that the whole thing was invented to celebrate the capture of a six-hundred-pound blue marlin some generations ago."

Local opinion suggests pineapple, lemon, and orange as the "several kinds of fruit juice" and Falernum as "the agent." A dash of bitters is essential; and some propose a syrup made from guava jelly as a sweetener. Some say, however, that a modest hint of red pepper is good, in case the mixture of dark and light rums that is central to the project seems to lack sufficient power.

Arlette Brisson, while not charting the minefields of New York "tables of ten," or grooming for her ongoing appearance on the "Ten Best Dressed" list, is a frequent weekender on Bermuda's rock beaches, where she prefers to let the hospitable planters prepare the punch while she suns at the seashore.

She finds that the flat wave-worn reef rocks make a perfect place to picnic in solitary "shipwrecked" splendor.

While preparing to be rescued by her host's impeccable and talented staff, she may study an

Arlette Brisson

antique copy of Philip's General Atlas for other alluring island spots for a shipwreck. Her picnic basket includes several rums to sample, a purely decorative loaf of bread, and some quite inedible beach grapes picked from behind the rocks.

Her lunch will be served on an Este ceramic tray and dishes in Tiffany's "Magnolia" pattern.

There is an antique English sailing mug of ample volume for iced beer imported from her native Belgium. The trompe l'oeil asparagus box protects the salt and pepper shakers and mustard pot from the breeze.

Lunch will begin with a chilled, lemon-accented fresh asparagus mousse followed by cold wiener schnitzels, the exact size and thickness of silver dollars, and served with three onion dishes.

There will be onions baked with raisins and olive oil, a salad of wilted onion rings and hard-boiled egg slices dressed with a sour cream dressing, and a faintly sweet corn and onion tart not at all dissimilar to a quiche.

A bowl of homemade fresh pineapple ice cream will complete the "shipwreck" lunch and may just be improved by a shot of "gold" poured over it to celebrate another day in the sun.

Her picnic basket includes several rums to sample, a purely decorative loaf of bread, and some quite inedible beach grapes picked from behind the rocks.

Nantucket

ince Christopher Hussy took the first whale off Nantucket in 1712, that tranquil little island lying less than thirty miles off the southern shore of Cape Cod has been associated with ship captains and adventurers on the high seas. During the eighteenth century, whaling and trade brought the island to rank with Boston and Salem as a leading commercial center, and brought unhoped-for prosperity to its sailing families.

Of its many handsome ship captain's houses, the most noble, now the home of Mrs. Allan Melhado, was built by Jared Coffin in 1820 from plans drawn up in London. Its bricks were brought back as ballast in Coffin's ships from England.

In the dining room of the Melhado house a whaling mural painted in 1927 by Stanley Roland commemorates the daring exploits of Captain Coffin.

The informal summer lunches given there are a tribute to the Nantucket summer colony's gracious and conservative life-style.

The cold lobsters will be served with a salad of new potatoes, celery, hard-boiled eggs, and cucumbers mixed with a dressing of equal halves of fresh mayonnaise and sour cream seasoned with a few capers and a bit of roughly chopped parsley, and dill pickle. The lobsters will be followed by green garden salad and a selection of American cheeses.

The dishes at lunch are antique Wedgwood. The flat silver is Tiffany's "Windham." The crystal and furniture, like the style of the house, are nineteenth-century English.

Victorian Staffordshire figures from Mrs. Melhado's extensive collection hold roses and astilbes from the garden.

After lunch, tea and cakes will be served in the front parlor, in front of one of the only four

Mrs. Allan Melhado

known copies of Dufour's "Captain Cook" wallpaper printed in 1804 and placed in the house of Jared Coffin.

The Portuguese cakes and cookies, so typical of Cape Cod and Nantucket, are reminders of Portuguese fishermen's frequent visits to the Grand Banks in search of codfish.

The "Captain Cook" wallpaper commemorates Cook's discovery of the Hawaiian Islands in 1778 while sailing from the Society Islands to the west coast of North America in search of the mythical Northwest Passage.

The close connection of Nantucket and Hawaii may not be evident to the luncheon guests, but the hostess will be happy to explain the significance of the native dances in the Dufour scenic paper.

They portray the Makahiki New Year's feast of the agricultural fertility god, Lono, in January 1779.

Returning to "The Sandwich Islands" for a second time to trade English iron nails for Hawaiian pigs and other provisions, and to have a bit of rest and recreation for himself and his men, Captain Cook arrived, for the second year in a row, in the midst of the Makahiki. The feather-crowned chief, Kalaniopuu, presided over the festivities. The natives took the visiting

Victorian Staffordshire figures from Mrs. Melhado's
extensive collection hold roses and astilbes from the garden

captain for Lono incarnate and feted the English in high island style.

Unfortunately, by February 14, 1779, the party got rowdy and Cook overstepped his bounds when he tried to discipline Kalaniopuu, uncle of Kamehameha I. That was the last of Captain James Cook, R.N.

In 1819 the great Hawaiian King Kamehameha died. A few months later American ships captured the first whales of Hawaii. Captain Coffin's fine new house was built at this time, attesting to his involvement in the following fifty years of New England domination of the Hawaiian whaling industry.

The Nantucket summer colony's gracious and conservative life-style

The Portuguese cakes and cookies, so typical of
Cape Cod and Nantucket

The Island of Staten

The Alice Austen house, Clear Comfort, stands on the northeast shore of Staten Island, more or less at the spot where astonished Algonquin Indians watched Henry Hudson's *Half Moon* sail into the Narrows one peaceful day in 1609.

The view is now spanned by a bridge named for the island's first European visitor, Giovanni da Verrazano, who arrived eighty-five years before Hudson. Here, where Algonquins once gaped in wonder, the tennis-playing friends of Staten Island–born Mario Buatta now lunch in tranquil splendor.

Were the ghosts of great documentary photographer and tennis player Alice Austen and the commander of the Hessian mercenaries who lived here during the Revolutionary War to walk down the lawn, they would come upon Mr. Buatta's Victorian wicker table and chairs set for lunch. Tiffany's "Faneuil" flat silver and Este "Leaf" pattern buffet plates grace the table. Crystal tennis ball paperweights are there to secure the antique lace tablecloth against an unexpected breeze.

There are bloody Marys for all and corn chips in a center bowl of Tiffany French faïence.

Mr. Buatta's lunch will begin with thin finger sandwiches of smoked salmon, cucumber, watercress, and cream cheese followd by soup plates of sea scallops and lobster meat "à la nage" in a creamy broth with asparagus tips, thin carrot sticks, shredded leeks, and young French beans.

For dessert there will be meringue shells half-filled with caramel-flavored "crème pâtissière" and generously topped with fresh peach slices.

Looking away from the Verrazano Bridge, the tennis enthusiasts will see the New York harbor once so beautifully photographed by Miss Austen from the same spot.

Mario Buatta

If ever I would have to think about having a house in the country, this would be the ideal setting. The house has untold charm. It was very much overgrown when we knew it as children. I've seen film clips of Alice's little garden parties for her friends and her black-and-white cats. All the furniture was auctioned off. Now they are trying to find the buyers, to ask them to donate it back to the house so that it can take on some of its original form again

Mario Buatta

Morning Glory Luncheon

The evanescence of morning glories at midday offer "a pleasant moment and a wonderful memory, and that's just the light, fleeting feeling that a good meal with family or friends should have," explains Mrs. T. Murray McDonnell.

At the McDonnell estate in Peapack, New Jersey, the focus is first on family and then on an "interest in nature, in gardening and flowers."

When the morning glories are in bloom, brunch will be served in a rail-fenced section of garden. This area is devoted to a lively mix of herbs, vegetables, and flowers and is guarded by a fashionably dressed scarecrow of the hostess's own design.

The table will be laid with a red-and-white country "check" and Tiffany's traditional Tyrolean "Biedermeier" earthenwares. These come from the picturesque Austrian mountain lake village of Gmunden, well known to artists and designers, where flowers play as important a role in daily life and design as they do at Mrs. McDonnell's.

The flat silver is Tiffany's "Faneuil." The handblown glass soup bowls and wineglasses are all designed and made by Mrs. McDonnell's talented and celebrated son-in-law, Simon Pearce.

With the exception of the hot yellow cornmeal muffins, everything for brunch comes from the garden, "picked moments before arriving at the table, and eaten before it all curls up from the sun."

The Simon Pearce bowls hold cold borscht made from garden-grown beets and herbs. The "Biedermeier" compote holds high a salad — almost too decorative to eat — of garden asparagus, baby zucchinis, several lettuces, arugula, green onions, tomatoes, and dill weed.

For dessert there is an openwork bowl of fresh green figs and blackberries.

Mrs. T. Murray McDonnell

During brunch, the evolution and improvement of the garden's constantly changing design will be discussed.

"The garden," Mrs. McDonnell points out to her guests, "just continues to grow and change its patterns yearly, like a quilt that's never finished. It has the convivial family atmosphere that I enjoy."

"A pleasant moment and a wonderful memory, and that's just the light, fleeting feeling that a good meal with family or friends should have "

Fête Louis-Philippe

In 1797 during the height of the Directory's second "Reign of Terror," the twenty-four-year-old Duc d'Orléans spent four months touring the newly independent United States with his two younger brothers, the Duc de Montpensier and the Comte de Beaujolais. He visited Mount Vernon and the George Washingtons, who would have commiserated with the three boys on the loss of their father, Philippe-Égalité, only four years before during the first "Reign of Terror." He spent some days among the Indians at "Tellico" and then wrote a curious volume entitled *Journal de mon voyage d'Amérique*. Thirty-three years later the Restauration brought the Duc d'Orléans to the French throne as King Louis-Philippe and thereby made him the first foreign head of state to have visited the United States. Some 180-odd years later his great-great-granddaughter, Princess Chantal of France, and her husband, the Baron François-Xavier de Sambucy returned to America to live quietly with their three children, Axel, Alexandre, and Kildine in a New Jersey town.

Here, in their comfortable turn-of-the-century house surrounded by souvenirs of the French royal family, the princess enjoys entertaining friends from nearby New York and relations from Paris.

Her dining room is furnished with chairs designed by her father, Henri, Comte de Paris, the pretender to the French throne, and covered in flowered embroidery of the princess's own design and fabrication.

Her tables are set with French porcelains reproduced by the princess for Tiffany & Co. from originals once belonging to Louis-Philippe and made by Sèvres in the late 1840s for all the royal châteaux.

H.R.H. Chantal de France

Along with the "Service des Châteaux Louis-Philippe" there is "Chrysanthemum" flat silver and "Nemours" Baccarat crystal.

The centerpiece is a Louis XV–style Puiforcat tureen in vermeil.

Vermeil pheasants from the royal family's estate in Portugal wander decoratively among the table's bouquets of pink garden roses. French royal portraits of Mary Stuart of Scotland, wife of François II, and of Marguerite de Valois, first wife of Chantal's ancestor Henri IV, survey the setting.

Dinners at the New Jersey house tend toward simple French food: a "salade panaché" of fine French green beans and fresh "fois gras d'oie," a light Parmesan and Gruyère cheese soufflé made by the hostess. These are followed by a rolled roast of veal "larded" with black truffles and served with chanterelles bordelaise. For dessert there is an enormous bowl of the princess's favorite chocolate mousse.

Vermeil pheasants from the royal family's estate in Portugal

Fruits and Fruit Tisane

Europe's courts of the eighteenth century replaced the overpowering architecture and ceremonies of their predecessors with small, domestically scaled, and exquisitely refined luxuries. They dressed superbly and conversed brilliantly as they sipped tea or chocolate from flowered porcelains in the most sybaritic interiors imaginable. Those too were sometimes lacquered and flowered in emulation of porcelain. They knew about the "douceur de vivre" — the sweetness of life. As Sir Kenneth Clark pointed out in his essay *Civilisation*, "nobody but a sourpuss or a hypocrite would deny that this was an agreeable way of life."

After over a decade as editor-in-chief of *House & Garden*, Mary Jane Pool knows as much as anyone about the domestic pleasures that make life sweet. And anyone familiar with Mary Jane Pool's writings on "The Gardens of Venice" knows that she is in complete accord with the infinite grace of Venetian life as lived in its great eighteenth-century interiors.

Her high-ceilinged rooftop pavilion above New York's East River — New York's "Grand Canal" — evokes Venice with all its luxurious attention to detail. Here, the summer lunch menu will share the setting's authenticity.

The meal will begin with a salad of shredded celery, mushrooms, and Gruyère, topped with "tartufi bianchi" and dressed with balsamic vinegar and "very green" olive oil.

The main course will be thin green tagliarini gratinéed in a rich béchamel flavored with nutmeg, Parmesan, bits of prosciutto and fine-cut filets of ripe tomato.

There will be San Pellegrino water and "no wine, nothing dangerous," says the hostess, "but for dessert and after the meal there will be warm and fragrant and digestive fruit tisanes."

The tisanes begin with packaged "mandarn orange tea" brewed with a stick of cinnamon

Mary Jane Pool

added to the pot. Guests then add fresh citrus slices or, for sweetened tisanes, sticks of ginger or of candied orange, lemon, or grapefruit peel.

"I also love finger things," Mary Jane Pool observes, and there will be chocolate twigs, chocolate truffles, grapes, and strawberries in silver Tiffany baskets.

The table base is a gold and silver "mecca"-finished neo-classic Italian urn. It is set with "Chrysanthemum" flatware and Tiffany's Bing & Grøndahl "Nymphalidae" series dessert plates whose basket edge coordinates with the other "table furniture."

The tea service is Royal Berlin decorated with "Saxon" flowers.

The lacquered flowered commmode, like the portrait it holds, is eighteenth-century Venetian, as is the "dolphin" mirror.

*They dressed superbly and conversed brilliantly as they sipped
tea or chocolate from flowered porcelains in the most sybaritic
interiors imaginable*

Russian Table d'Hôte

round twenty-five years ago a thin red-pink folio cookbook entitled *Wild Raspberries* appeared in New York. The text was by Suzie Frankfurt and the handcolored illustrations by Andy Warhol. Its rambunctious recipes for such arch cuisine offerings as "Seared Roebuck," "Baked Hawaii," and "A & P Surprise" caused little stir in high culinary circles. In fact, not one of the first edition's forty-five proto–Pop Art masterpiece copies ever left the art world, where the Warhol-Frankfurt recipe for "Two Day Old Cake" became and remains a legend. More than a few art "groupies" over the years have been guilty of religiously following Suzie Frankfurt's instructions to slice a stale supermarket cake in two and "soak for exactly 36 hours in ½ cup rum, 2½ tablespoons confectioner's sugar, and ½ cup water."

If the cookbook's then unknown authors lacked sound culinary credentials, they brought to their project a soaring appetite for fun and roaring chic that makes this thin volume thick with the cultural wealth commonly called "entertainment value."

The abundantly talented Suzie Frankfurt is better known today as a leader in the realm of interior design than for her writings on food. Happily, she acknowledges a lack of any deeply felt taste for cooking, as she so adroitly demonstrates in this classically Pop recipe for "Piglet" found in *Wild Raspberries:*

"Contact Trader Vic's and order a 40-pound suckling pig to serve 15. Have Hanley take the Carey Cadillac to the side entrance and receive the pig at exactly 6:45. Rush home immediately and turn on the open spit for 50 minutes. Remove and garnish with fresh crabapples."

Since "Piglet" was published, Trader Vic's has left its smart Savoy Plaza location, replaced in 1968 by the General Motors Building, home of the Cadillac but not of the take-out suckling

Suzie Frankfurt

pig. Suzie Frankfurt has moved to an Upper East Side town house, which her knowing hand has transformed into a miniature neo-classic Tsarist Russian palace.

Here, in the filtered and dappled half light of the Belle Époque French chandelier, guests dine seated on Austrian Biedermeier chairs at an Italian Empire table. The flowered and gilded dinner plates are 1830 Restauration Sèvres from Mrs. Frankfurt's mother's collection. The flat silver is from Tiffany's, and the early nineteenth-century Moor guarding the entrance with a bouquet of pretty flowers is from Venice.

Whereas *Wild Raspberries* proposed a "Salade de Alf Landon" "as a first course at political dinners in the 30's," Suzie Frankfurt proposes a Russian fish stew as a first course in the East Seventies. In profligate Tsarist fashion, the stew avoids ingredients native to Russia in favor of extravagant quantities of capers, green peppercorns, and thinly sliced pimiento-filled green olives as flavoring for a praiseworthy mixture of cubes of barely cooked fresh salmon, sautéed celery, and white onion in an equal blend of chicken stock and light cream.

After the salmon there may be a boneless roast of veal with prunes baked in the pan juices and yellow summer squash baked with an herbed cornbread stuffing.

After dinner, guests will drift up to one of the house's more intimate private rooms. There, a dish of mixed berries will be offered with coffee and one of the hostess's favorite dacquoise cakes filled with a thick praline cream and decorated with marzipan bows and flowers.

The coffee will be served in a gold-and-white 1820s Russian porcelain pot on a Tiffany "Chrysanthemum" tray, the berries in a silver trompe l'oeil dish made in St. Petersburg in 1883.

"My life to date is a combination of Pompeii and Coney Island, which is just great," says Suzie Frankfurt, "because that's what America is all about."

A soaring appetite for fun and roaring chic

In profligate Tsarist fashion, the Russian fish stew avoids
ingredients native to Russia

A Vermeil, Vermeil Special Brunch

t dining boards and designing boards, the edible shoot of the asparagus officinalis is a welcome guest. From the streamlined geometry of the tender green tip down its slender stalk to the pale mauve liliaceous feet, asparagus is a winner. Its shoots regularly inspire ceramists and enamelers to imitate their forms in trompe l'oeil boxes, plates, bowls, candlesticks, and bric-a-brac.

At table, despite Ms. Isabella Beeton's observance that "it belongs to the class of luxurious rather than necessary food," and that "it is light and easily digested but is not very nutritious," asparagus finds a welcome place. It may be served in a mousse or a pudding, a soufflé, a soup or a sauce, or simply steamed and served with melted butter or almost any variation of a hollandaise, mayonnaise, or vinaigrette.

Adolfo, whose suits and dresses could also be termed luxurious rather than necessary, dressed his brunch table with French faïence asparagus trompe l'oeil boxes from Tiffany's.

Real asparagus will be served at brunch on Tiffany's Private Stock "Carousel Chinois" china and eaten with Tiffany's "Hampton" vermeil flat silver.

The meal will begin with thinly sliced Norwegian smoked salmon topped with equally thin lemon slices thickly spread with black malossol caviar.

This will be accompanied by tiny glasses of ice-cold vodka and followed by the steamed asparagus served with a classic quiche Lorraine.

At another meal, asparagus tips might be successfully mixed with the minced ham and onions

Adolfo

in the quiche's egg custard filling, in the manner of an old-fashioned Victorian asparagus pudding.

For dessert there will be another classic, a crème caramel in all its simplicity served with champagne in Tiffany's elegant "Honeycomb" cut crystal flutes.

The table's centerpiece is a Royal Berlin porcelain tureen in the "Breslau Castle" pattern, first made for Frederick the Great in the late eighteenth century. The tureen is surrounded by small bouquets of lily of the valley which coordinate with their liliaceous asparagus cousins.

From an easel standing on an antique black-and-gold Chinese blanket chest, a portrait of a pug dog supervises brunch.

Adolfo's pugs feel this "vermeil, vermeil special brunch" is too much gilding the liliaceous for their taste.

"They don't particularly like what we're eating," their owner comments. "They like something else — usually cold boiled chicken."

"It belongs to the class of luxurious rather than necessary food"

Luncheon at Chanel, Inc.

If you were born without wings, do nothing to prevent their growing," wisely advised Coco Chanel; and, whether they unfurled at birth or grew later, no one can say, but Chanel flew higher and further on her wings than any fashion figure of this century.

Complete naturalness characterized her style. Her "wings" were simple black sheaths in crêpe de Chine and little white collars. Was it all part of the reverse snobbism of the twenties, or, as Paul Poiret called it, "poverty de luxe"? Whatever it was, it left no branch of twentieth-century fashion untouched.

If the Chanel style continues to flourish over one hundred years after the birth of Gabrielle Chanel, it is largely due to the vision and talents of Kitty D'Alessio, the American president of Chanel, Inc., who presides over the Chanel empire from a black-lacquered office forty-four stories above Central Park. Possessed of what Chanel designer Karl Lagerfeld calls her "view of the whole thing," which is simply her unerring instinct that recalls the incomparable "Mademoiselle," D'Alessio has brought the house of Chanel triumphantly into the 1980s following her own dictum, "Open the windows, let in the year we're living in."

Not one to fritter away the hours with the local luncheon set, Kitty D'Alessio enjoys stylishly simple business meals served in her own offices.

"You can accomplish so much more, like quickly getting to the point, than in a public place. To business people the privacy of staying in is so agreeable," she says, and adds, "What a great favor, too, to the host — not to have to go out."

Her round marble table, designed like all the furniture in her offices by Jay Spectre, is set with pale gray-green "Celadon" porcelain and Tiffany's understated "Salem" flat silver. Pet

Kitty D'Alessio

bronze birds by Diego Giacometti decorate the table along with a variety of miniature orchids and a modern sculpture.

Appealingly simple food will be served "because that's all working people eat," says the hostess.

Lunch will begin with a salad of thinly sliced tomatoes and salt-free mozzarella rounds garnished with basil, olive oil, vinegar, and freshly ground black pepper, and a few black olives for color contrast.

The entrée will be grilled sole, with lemon sections, followed by bowls of fresh cantaloupe sherbet served with gaufrettes imported from Brittany.

A choice of chilled white wine, still Evian mineral water, or fresh grapefruit juice will be offered with lunch.

Bottles of Chanel's legendary fragrance "No. 5" sit everywhere, the complexity of its 128 ingredients contrasting with the straightforward simplicity of the lunch.

Promotional materials lie about the room and serve as props to the serious business at hand.

"Much seriousness is required," Chanel observed, "to achieve the frivolous."

A salad of thinly sliced tomatoes and salt-free mozzarella rounds garnished with basil, olive oil, vinegar, and freshly ground black pepper, and a few black olives

An Outgrabeous Dinner

Were Lewis Carroll to meet today's quintessential New Yorker, he would probably rethink the judgment written in his diary of 1880: "I fear it is true that there are no children in America."

New York has evolved into the most post-Carrollian of towns. Here each sort and condition of thing "gyres and gimbles in the wabe," and "mome raths" are not the only ones among them to behave in an "outgrabeous" fashion. In New York, no fantasy is left unturned, and the manual that New Yorkers know every trick in is a reprint of Alice's *"Looking-Glass* book."

At Fifth Avenue dinners, if a few little touches of absurdity are not given full play, the "older children" at the table will feel that something necessary has been left out.

The last to ignore our Carrollian heritage, Design Director of Tiffany & Co., John Loring, one of Gotham's high priests of the decorative arts, sets a dinner table to bring smiles to the most jaded denizen of Wonderland. At table, the "Halcyon" china with its pastel flowers and ribbons on a gold-flecked cobalt blue background are of Mr. Loring's own mid-nineteenth-century-inspired design.

There will be no "beautiful soup, so rich and green," as lemons hollowed out and filled with red caviar have already been planted in a cold soup of jellied madrilene enriched with sour cream and flavored with dry sherry and paprika. The gold-and-raspberry-pink "Framboise Rose" soup plates were designed by Mr. Loring's predecessor at Tiffany's, Mr. Van Day Truex.

White wine is served in German crystal marriage goblets. Red wine and champagne will be served in Tiffany's exclusive "Nemours" Baccarat crystal stemware. The red wine decanter is also from the "Nemours" collection, as is the candlestick which has collapsed on the table under

John Loring

the weight of an opera-length strand of Tiffany's cultured pearls.

A few flowers are successfully kept in their places while others tip about and spill onto the table from Tiffany's Venetian and Bavarian crystal vases.

Cut crystal "diamond" paperweights prop themselves up on large linked gold bangles beside two rock crystal scarab rings by Donald Claflin; all from Tiffany's.

A "party cake" by Colette Peters is underpinned by three crystal balls. An Art Deco bronze perroquet by Édouard Marcel Sandoz stands by.

After the caviar soup, there will be a chicken, roasted with a great many black olives, a few sweet sausages, and the juice of two lemons. Before roasting, it has been thoroughly coated with olive oil and a mixture of tarragon, rosemary, black pepper, salt, and a goodly amount of grated lemon peel.

The chicken will be served with French green beans parboiled and sautéed with shallots and a pinch of whole thyme leaves. There will also be a purée of parsnips, white turnips, and celery.

The astounding cake, which has nothing to do with Alice's "very small cake, on which the words 'EAT ME' were beautifully marked in currants," is for dessert. All topsy-turvy and rocket-bursting with stars of enthusiasm, the cake is scarcely able to contain itself. And, were Alice there, she would tell it "with a merry laugh," "Sit up a little more stiffly, dear!" just in honor of being a New Yorker.

After the cake whose bourbon-flavored butter cream filling will complement the homemade bittersweet chocolate ice cream, there will be plenty of time to "fill up the glasses with treacle and ink, or anything else that is pleasant to drink; mix sand with the cider, and wool with the wine — and welcome [the evening] with ninety-times-nine!"

In New York, no fantasy is left unturned

Working My Way

Those who dine at L'Orangerie in Los Angeles, the Carlyle in Houston, Doubles, the Polo Bar, the new Cafe Pierre, or the Plaza Athénée in New York will recognize the grand and nuanced high style of Valerian Rybar of *Valerian Rybar Design Corp.*

Luxury, extravagance, and exhilarating contrasts of texture, materials, and scale mark Rybar interiors, not only in the public playgrounds of the privileged, but also in the locales of their domestic festivities.

The privileged are also often the private, and for working design discussions, Valerian Rybar favors lunches in his Madison Avenue offices and dinners in his Sutton Place flat, "rather than going out and being overheard by the next table where everyone listens to everything you say, which is not," he explains, "working my way."

The intimate living room of Valerian Rybar's apartment with its coral-red-velvet walls anchored by the glowing platform that he calls "my famous textured stainless steel floor" is the setting for working dinners with out-of-town clients.

An original Boulle "Mazarin" desk is set with Tiffany vermeil silverwares and a dazzling array of "objets de vertu." "When I do these things," says Rybar, "I take out objects I might keep in a closet or in another room and arrange them in different ways for different occasions."

Sitting on three volumes of a mock four-hundred-volume *Life of Valerian Rybar,* a powerfully beautiful seventeenth-century Florentine rock crystal and gilt bronze bust of Ferdinand de' Medici rules the table. Ferdinand, Grand Duke of Tuscany, sometime cardinal, great art connoisseur, and founder of the Villa Medici in Rome, was also a triumphant leader of the Tuscan Navy. In honor of his naval post, red wine is served in a Tiffany ship's decanter and

Valerian Rybar

drunk from oversized footed coupes in Florentine baroque fashion. Behind Ferdinand, Mount Vesuvius, framed in steel, obligingly erupts in the eighteenth-century painting.

In sharp contrast to Ferdinand, a nineteenth-century Viennese bronze monkey, stripped of his original polychroming and gilded by Rybar, sits looking for fleas at the foot of an English Regency candlestick, whose sea motifs continue the setting's theme.

A vase of Rothschild lilies is entirely at home on the table. Cracked lobsters fill a shell-footed bowl which Rybar found in a small antique shop in Oporto. Their shells pick up the coral red of the walls.

The cold lobsters will be served with a sauce of mixed fresh mayonnaise and heavy cream flavored with lemon juice, cayenne, and lots of finely chopped coriander leaves.

The main course will be brochettes of boneless baby lamb chops grilled aux herbes de Provence and accompanied by a tepid eggplant caviar.

The ginger-scented "crème bavaroise" is the only hint of the more northern taste of Ferdinand's wife, Christina of Lorraine.

An English sealing wax box holds ivory and vermeil measures and yardsticks, the "utensils" of Mr. Rybar's trade.

Red wine is served in a Tiffany ship's decanter and drunk from oversized footed coupes in Florentine baroque fashion

After the Opera

Being served up on a table decked in "bubble wrap" is enough to try the patience of an oyster; however, what bivalves find bothersome, less reactionary mortals find fun.

On the principle that having as much fun as possible is the point of entertaining, Jean-François Daigre of *Valerian Rybar & Daigre, Inc.*, has delighted Patinos, Rothschilds, and other social deities too party-going to mention at balls "Red" and "Oriental" at Ferrières and the Louvre.

From small-scaled beginnings in the early 1960s, when he caught the eye of Paris with his window displays at Christian Dior, Daigre has become a world leader in fête design.

The high hues of parties are right for parties, but at home Daigre proves that gray is gregarious.

A half-circle alcove in his apartment's "grisaille" entrance hall serves as a dining room for after-opera suppers.

In front of the stormy grays of a neo-classic seaside mural by Jan Rithamer, Jean-François Daigre skirts a round glass table with everyday "bubble wrap" and lights it from within.

The gentle welling light flows up through footed crystal plates and a footed fishbowl centerpiece all designed for Tiffany & Co. by Elsa Peretti. Crystal trumpet glasses by Josef Hoffmann hold champagne whose buoyant bubbles coordinate with the tablecloth.

A trompe l'oeil grisaille fish swims in the Peretti fish globe, and champagne sits in crushed ice in a Tiffany silver wave bowl. The flat silver is "Faneuil."

Bluepoint oysters on the half shell and seaweed garnished with mussels wait for guests to return from the Metropolitan Opera. The mussels, like the seaweed, were chosen for their

Jean-François Daigre

decorative rather than their comestible merits. The oysters, nestled on beds of crushed ice, are offered with lemon halves and a red wine vinegar, black pepper, and minced shallot "sauce poulette."

Cold roast pheasants will follow the oysters, served with a salad of blanched and chilled red cabbage slightly sweetened with dark brown sugar and accented with a few caraway seeds.

For dessert there will be a "compote tiède" of fresh halves of pears, apricots, plums, and black cherries poached in vintage port wine and served in crystal soup plates.

Late-eighteenth-century Piedmontese shield-back chairs and a porphyry-topped Directoire guéridon holding the champagne echo the neo-classic architecture of the mural's seaside pavilions, while the painted statuary carries out operatic abductions.

The diners' anecdotes at this grisaille supper will be "positivement grisantes."

Having as much fun as possible is the point of entertaining

Verveine

All credit for discovering that the stem, no matter how long, is not the most interesting part of a flower and that the budget, no matter how big, is not the most sacred feature of a party, goes to Marlo Phillips, New York's queen of flowers. The several scissors hanging about her person from curiously knotted cords and ribbons have hacked armies of high-flowering hybrids down to size; and her imagination and extravagance have made a hash of the most ambitious party budgets in the cosmos.

"I start by taking a lot of things I like and fortunately I have a lust for everything," says Marlo, revealing her secrets. "I lose myself in what I'm doing, become obsessed with ribbons and buttons and hatboxes and stuffed animals and dolls and snake plants and pussywillows and objects joined with flowers."

At a tea party set for her favorite stuffed Dormouse to entertain Alice, Marlo traces Alice's "fall" with a cascade of rose tulle spilling onto a tulle-covered table. A fantasy cake, like Alice's elixir, has "a sort of mixed flavour of cherry-tart, custard, pine-apple, roast turkey, toffy, and hot buttered toast."

For Alice's arrival, the conservatory is overflowing with bouquets from Marlo Flowers, Ltd., for that "fleeting flower zillion-dollar moment," as Marlo puts it.

"Flora Danica" cups and saucers and Tiffany's "Battersea" enamel and Private Stock porcelain boxes are strewn about with lavish abandon.

Marlo's pet dime-store-born Oriental finch Peter has come to the party, which will be lit by a galaxy of Tiffany candlesticks in both silver and porcelain. The verveine tea will be poured from Tiffany silver.

Marlo Phillips

Breakfast with the Doge

erenissima" is a name popularly given to Venice, however little serenity that city of artists and warriors, merchants and mischief-makers has known. The town of Titian and Tintoretto, Morosini and Marco Polo, Arlecchino and Pulcinella is a town of passion and event, of grandeur, comedy, carnival, and a lust for living out the details of daily life in the most sumptuous settings yet devised. Venice is a town of intelligence and sensuality, but not of serenity.

It has been said of John Saladino that whether designing interiors, furniture, gardens, or a party, "he has the remarkable ability to make the intelligent sensual." This is not surprising, as his mother is Venetian.

"The last gasp of ceremony in our lives," says Saladino, "the last ceremonial act in the twentieth century, is to sit down and dine. And to do it well, you have to bring passion to this small moment in time. Dining well is a gesture that should elevate us."

At a breakfast of fantasy, where Saladino sits down with the Doge of Venice to discuss the décor of a pageant honoring one of the four seasons, the table is set with "Celadon" porcelain honoring Venetian trade with China and Tiffany crystal honoring Venetian supremacy in glassmaking.

The flat silver is Tiffany's "Windham," honoring the county in eastern Connecticut which was the boyhood home of Charles Lewis Tiffany, who founded Tiffany & Co. in 1837.

In the manner of a late seventeenth-century baroque still life painting, the setting combines breads and fruits, the spare, simple elements of an Italian country breakfast, and elevates them to the world of art, transforming them into trophies and gemstones. The very humble,

John Saladino

elaborately presented, becomes the very grand.

Saladino colors his still life in pinks that slip away into mauve, grays, and other carefully calculated, soft, "aged" colors. An intricate network of transparencies and reflections furthers the intention.

Supporting the table's role as an altar to good living, a baldachin of silk taffeta is held aloft by four fluted wooden columns which crown the breakfast.

There are plenty of tuberoses whose heady perfume will remind the breakfasters of September nights and Venetian palace parties.

The traditional sweet, crescent-shaped "ciambelline alla Veneziana" and other breads in this staff-of-life-based meal are accompanied by fresh orange juice, a glass of light white wine from the hills northeast of Venice, and San Pellegrino water — "a product," Saladino observes, "the last Doge would not have been familiar with." There is also caffè latte which, Venetians observe, is "buono quando è caldo e gratis."

Here, in every detail, is a passion for luxury that evokes what "everyone loves about Venice," says John Saladino, "the spectacle, the glitter, the pastry of its architecture, and the allegros and andantes of its ceremonies."

*"The last gasp of ceremony in our lives, the last ceremonial act in
the twentieth century, is to sit down and dine"*

L'Or de l'Orangerie

By crossing the Parterres du Midi at Versailles and descending the cyclopean stone staircase known as the Cent Marches, one gains access to L'Orangerie. In the time of Louis XIV, this masterpiece of Mansart garden design housed some two thousand boxed orange trees and half again that many decorative shrubs, some of which still survive.

Access to L'Orangerie at New York's Le Cirque is gained by crossing the lobby of the Mayfair Regent Hotel, then making a quick right through a corner of the lounge. The maneuver is permitted only to those with an invitation to one of the blatantly elitist social events that take place in this inner sanctum of Sirio Maccioni's legendary restaurant.

Here, with the aid of twenty-one cooks, three pastry chefs, and occasionally the help of his three sons, Mauro, Marco, and Morio, Maccioni serves the rich, the chic, the powerful, the famous, and their following, with his personal brand of haute Franco-Italian cuisine whose absolute perfection discourages explanation.

The décors of the luncheons and suppers and dinner dances given in L'Orangerie change rapidly. At a typically New York fun-raising dinner, the round tables of the columned and mirrored room might be skirted with gold lamé cloths "planted" with sterling silver palm candlesticks from Tiffany & Co. and brass gilt palm trees from Regency England. Beneath the palms' golden fronds, collections of Royal Berlin porcelain birds, also from Tiffany & Co., enliven the place settings, thoroughly enjoying their golden cage.

The china is "Stampino," a Tiffany edition of the stenciled blue-and-white floral patterns used on the first Florentine porcelains of the eighteenth century. They are now made near Sirio Maccioni's hometown in Tuscany. The flatware is "Windham."

Sirio Maccioni

Reinforcing the tropical motif, fronded porcelain pots hold red anthurium flowers. Tiffany porcelain and enamel boxes hold party favors.

The champagne before the meal will be served with trays of "tapenade de caviar," made by spreading rounds of homemade "baguette" bread with eggplant caviar, covering this with a paper-thin slice of ripe tomato, and topping the whole thing with fresh black caviar.

To begin supper, there will be a choice of one of Le Cirque's two great dishes made with American foie gras: "coeur de truffe sous le cendre au foie gras de New York," a whole black truffle robed in New York State foie gras and served hot in a puff pastry shell; or "médaillons de foie gras américains," with caramelized apple sections.

After the foie gras, there will be a light "court bouillon de homard" with ample pieces of Maine lobster meat.

The main course will be Le Cirque's "selle de veau farci aux pistaches" served with braised Belgian endives and artichoke hearts filled with spring peas. The saddle of veal is boned, stuffed with chopped, cooked spinach and mushrooms, pistachio nuts, and roasted.

For dessert there will be a "soufflé aux poires, sauce chocolat amer".

The foie gras and then the lobster bouillon will be served with a cold Friuli 1983, a Luna dei Feldi di Rovere della Luna.

For the roast veal, neither the reserves of Château Gruaud-Larose 1865 nor Château Latour 1893 resting peacefully in Le Cirque's cellar will be tapped. Instead, there will be a 1959 Nuits Saint-Georges, cuvée des Sires de Vergy, in all its unpretentious excellence.

"With dessert," Sirio observes, "I can offer all the Château d'Yquem you can imagine. You can go wild with the dessert wines on the list, but I personally like a wine from one of the small Lipari Islands, fifty kilometers off the coast of Sicily, the 'Malvasia delle Lipari Tipo Passito 1983' from Salina. It's a wine of meditation."

An invitation to one of the blatantly elitist social events that take place in this inner sanctum of Sirio Maccioni's legendary restaurant

Souper Après le Bal Masqué

With the exception of the ground floor, the entire house at 3 East Fifty-second Street is occupied by a painter's studio of operatic proportions. Here Bernard Lamotte entertained an upper-crust Bohème that included show business celebrities such as Greta Garbo and Jean Gabin, as well as the sometime painter and culinary genius Charles Masson, who would later make this address famous as La Grenouille.

Lamotte's dinners were spirited events focused on a robust French country cuisine prepared by Lamotte himself and animated by an air of Gallic revelry. All this was watched over approvingly by the bust of the house saint, "Saint Zano," which stood on the studio's mantelpiece.

Today the studio houses the office and wine "cellar" of the restaurant La Grenouille, supervised by Madame Gisèle Masson, who with her sons, Charles and Philippe, maintains the same high tone of excellence set by her husband for New York's culinary establishment.

Downstairs, paintings by Lamotte and the Charles Massons Junior and Senior hang above La Grenouille's red plush banquettes. Here, the privileged, the celebrated, and the hopelessly enamored of fine French food dine beneath lavish floral architectures. At a favorite corner table Gisèle Masson, returning from a masked ball, might please herself and a friend with a light supper.

In the warm filtered light of one of La Grenouille's Art Nouveau table lamps, Madame Masson's black feather mask by Alexandre is discarded. She places it beside the setting's Imari bone china and Mason's ironstone Imari ginger jar from Tiffany & Co.

In the kitchen a Tiffany French faïence plateau, painted in the rayonnant style of Rouen,

Gisèle Masson

holds sea urchins, malpeque oysters, and bigorneaux, all waiting to be served as the appetizer.

The "fruits de mer" will be followed by a "consommé d'écrevisse en gelée" and then by a "poulet au gingembre" which Madame Masson explains is "un peu exotique et donne envie de boire beaucoup de champagne."

The supper will conclude with a "soupe aux fruits rouges."

"C'est un souper galant," explains the hostess. "Intime. Romantique. Un plaisir un peu passé, mais un plaisir à ramener. Faire un souper, c'est faire une nourriture de rêve.

"It must sparkle with la luxe totale."

"C'est un souper galant. Intime. Romantique"

Dinner for One, Champagne for Two

Louis Suë and André Mare were two of the greatest designers of 1920s Art Deco. In the furniture, objects, and interiors conceived at their "Compagnie des Arts Français," they collaborated with a brilliant lineup of artists, including Maillol, Despiau, Dufrène, de la Fresnay, and Marinot. With them, Suë et Mare built upon the unshakable foundations of Louis XIV and Louis XV style, but brought to the art of interior design a debonair, dapper, and thoroughly modern urbanity that, today, remains a triumph of twentieth-century civilization.

"We wish any handsome furnishing of former periods," they said, "to be at home with our works, to be received like an ancestor and not like an intruder."

Restaurateur Augustin Paege is as debonair and dapper as the Suë et Mare furnishings that keep him good company in his New York Deco apartment. He would agree with his two spiritual ancestors that civilization starts at the top of all things "rich and rare" and "as perfect as possible."

Away for a moment from the urbanities of his Box Tree restaurant and its highly civilized clientele, the aristocratic Bulgarian-born New Yorker chooses to dine alone in the company of his splendid collection of Art Deco objects and furnishings.

There is a pervasive air of civility to the scene. Its extreme and studied elegance in no way prevents its being very unpretentious, very private.

The Suë et Mare thuja wood table with its characteristic, powerfully carved cabriole legs is

Augustin Paege

set with Tiffany's "Hampton" flat silver and "Celadon" porcelain. There are fluted silver column candlesticks and an Art Deco silver coffee set, both from Tiffany & Co., as is the silver-and-crystal bud vase, designed by Elsa Peretti, which holds a single stem of freesias.

Although Suë et Mare decorated the *Île-de-France*, Paege's screen with its inlays of audaciously varied grains and patterns is from the first-class smoking room of the *Normandie*.

The dining-room chair is by Suë et Mare and wears its original Aubusson upholstery.

The "stockpot" soup tureen in sterling silver is by Tiffany's.

Dinner will be a single dish, a "fricassée des fruits de mer" made with a rich base of fish stock, fresh tomatoes, leeks, carrots, celery, garlic, onions, lemon juice, red pepper, salt, and fresh herbs. To this, clams, oysters, mussels, and lobsters will be added with abandon.

There will be a Chassagne-Montrachet 1982 to accompany the seafood and "the true gourmet's most common delight," a large piece of fresh baked country bread.

"When a gentleman dines alone," explains Augustin Paege, "he doesn't fuss around. He practically eats out of the pot — plenty of one good thing and a piece of good bread. It's enough.

"The point is to be able to make the evening into whatever he wants, to give himself an invigorating emotional uplift and then go out and radiate a great good feeling about himself.

"Then," he says, "he goes out and doesn't come home alone."

"Plenty of one good thing and a piece of good bread.
It's enough"

Holiday Fantasy Breakfast

With a wondrously unshackled sense of luxury, Mrs. John Gutfreund plays a Russian variation on the time-honored theme of breakfast in bed.

The breakfast features a single dish, fresh beluga malossol caviar, which Mrs. Gutfreund serves with sour cream and boiled potatoes.

"A potato is the only thing totally right with caviar," she points out. "It's simple; it's normal; it's the best marriage. It evokes New Year's Eve at St. Moritz and a whole life-style that can't be bettered."

The potatoes and caviar arrive on a silver gallery tray accompanied by a silver teapot and other silver utensils and ornaments, all from Tiffany & Co.'s silver collections.

The laces which deck the 1880s American brass bed with abandoned opulence are from Mrs. Gutfreund's collection of antique textiles. They include perfectly preserved nineteenth-century French laces from Alençon, Lille, and Chantilly as well as English lace from Bedfordshire, Buckinghamshire, and Coggeshall in Essex, and an Irish yardage or two from Carrickmacross.

At the foot of the bed an eighteenth-century silver bust of Catherine the Great sits on a unique nineteenth-century bronze doré table with a "textile collector's" silk collage top.

The tea will be served in Russian style in crystal mugs from Tiffany & Co. and stirred with Tiffany silver spoons in the Renaissance Revival pattern "San Lorenzo," introduced by Tiffany's in Russia's last "imperial" year, 1916. Behind the brass headboard a handpainted window shade by Michael Murdola depicts a Russian garden in winter.

To brighten the morning there is a miniature pine tree ornamented with fresh flowers and miniature gift boxes. A bag of Tiffany gift coins, sitting beneath the tree, is provided for after-breakfast shopping.

Mrs. John Gutfreund

Christmas Eve Dinner on Eaton Square

stée Lauder's femininity and her sure hand with the scents and shades of beauty have brought glamour to the lives of millions.

At Estée Lauder's fabled dinner parties, she sits at the head of her table just as she sits at the head of her empire, ruling it with charm, authority, and an unwavering conviction that her own sense of luxury and personal style are very much worth the offering.

At a Christmas Eve dinner for eight at her "flat" in London's fashionable Eaton Square, her table is covered with crimson silk damask and vermeiled silverwares from Tiffany & Co.

A topiary tree decked with antique silver baubles and gold ribbons announces the season, and her gift boxes at every place are wrapped in Estée Lauder Christmas paper.

Mrs. Lauder successfully combines contemporary "Rock Cut" crystal, Regency "Palm" vermeil, and Georgian "Baluster" silver candlesticks. Mixed stemware patterns carry on the theme of eclectic chic, as do the mixed "Hampton" and "Olympian" Tiffany flatwares.

Dinner will be served on a mixture of Tiffany's Private Stock patterns, including "Halcyon," "Cirque Chinois," and "Coeur Fleur," already represented on the table by the caviar-filled porcelain eggs beside the menus at each place.

After a frothy "consommé de volaille à la chiffonade" there will be individual hot lobster soufflés, English filet of beef "en croûte" with a savory purée of "pissenlit" and "oseille."

A salad of Belgian endives with red wine sauce will precede the traditional French yule-log Christmas cake, eaten with champagne.

Later, more little cakes with fondant icing follow with yet more champagne.

Estée Lauder

Un Thé Intimement
Néo-Classique

Strengthened rather than intimidated by the daunting shadow of her father's protean talents, Paloma Picasso shares his courage to be totally and publicly original.

Her own stylish visual sense with its smartly harnessed energy has revolutionized the look of late-twentieth-century jewelry through her designs for Tiffany & Co.

Her love of costume and "dressing up as something to offer other people" has thrice earned her the title of "Best Dressed Woman in the World."

Although it has been said that "Paloma Picasso has an unrivaled understanding of the red, black, and white look," it is a soundly schooled taste for generous scale, strong color, geometric form, and glowing surface that characterizes and ensures the success of her designs.

Paloma Picasso designs are as classic as they are original, and the classicism that unifies them recurs in the neo-imperial elegance of her Park Avenue salon.

The interior's aesthetic forebears include Sergei Diaghilev and Léon Bakst, Gabrielle Chanel, Andrea Sansovino, the Wiener Werkstaette, the Emperor Hadrian, Jean-Michel Frank, Andrea Palladio, and Mariano Fortuny, a lineup to intimidate the shy or inhibited.

The airy neo-Georgian salon's common denominator is black: black furniture, black statuary, black objects, black fringes, all pushed to the limits of their graphic possibilities in contrast to the fire-orange glazed chintz curtains which put the Paloma Picasso signature on this memorable interior.

Devoted to dining out with her husband, playwright Rafael López-Sánchez, Paloma Picasso

Paloma Picasso López

nevertheless has a fondness for elaborate tea parties, usually offered to a single guest.

A seventeenth-century Italian "scagliola" marble tabletop painted with dancing Roman deities holds an opulent variety of sweets.

There are hot sugared brioches, and meringues filled with almond-flavored custard topped with raspberries, both on Tiffany vermeil plates. There is also a silver basket of classic toast. A late nineteenth-century Russian silver trompe l'oeil basket found in Venice presents "Palmiers," whose neo-classic design enhances the setting.

A Victorian English glass-and-silver butter tub and cookie barrel hold still more sweets. A Tiffany crab candlestick holds a single, perfect delphinium blossom.

Tea is served from Tiffany silver in Tiffany Private Stock porcelain cups whose green and gold spottings were inspired by an eighteenth-century Russian chintz.

The table linens in Greek Revival style are late nineteenth-century Czechoslovakian. The other porcelains are Private Stock patterns.

On hot New York summer days, a tea at Paloma Picasso's is not restricted to tea alone. Both fresh lemonade and fresh orangeade are offered in antique Norman cider flasks from Rouen, as well as chilled red and white Italian wines in antique cut green Bristol glass decanters.

The wines and orangeade keep cool in an ice-filled seventeenth-century French brass font protected by a massive Istrian marble lion from Venice.

From its vantage point atop a Renaissance marble column, a Roman Janus looks both ways while a Pompeian faun flees the scene. The black-and-silver Russian Art Deco armchairs will probably not be used. The hostess and her guest will prefer to sit on the polished floor for tea while they discuss design projects and take notes with a Tiffany silver "quill" pen.

How well John Milton catches the mood of this delightful and charmingly innocent life-style: "A perpetual feast of nectar'd sweets, where no crude surfeit reigns."

Elaborate tea parties, usually offered to a single guest

A Louisiana Christmas on the Bayou

rand Chénier Camp in Louisiana is the scene of "a Long tradition": the Christmas supper of Louisiana's leading family, orchestrated by Mrs. Russell Long.

The menu begins with "shrimp rémoulade": fresh Gulf shrimp in a sauce of pounded hard-cooked egg yolk, Dijon mustard, salt, cayenne, olive oil, wine vinegar, and fresh tarragon leaves.

The shrimp are followed by "duck gumbo" served with "Louisiana wild pecan rice."

The gumbo is made by browning quartered ducks, then boiling them with celery, onions, red peppers, and more than a few pods of okra.

Supper concludes with a French Christmas "croquembouche" and a Creole-Hispanic "café brûlot," native to Louisiana's Spanish West Florida and the "Cajun" Plaquemine Parish. The necessary supply of Louisiana pecan pralines sits on a Tiffany silver tray.

The Long's French country pine table is set with cobalt blue and pure "All White" porcelains from Tiffany & Co. The crystal trumpet glasses are "Sharon," and the flat silver is named for Louisiana's sometime dancing master, French teacher, art and fencing instructor, taxidermist, sign painter, steamboat muralist, and great naturalist painter John James Audubon.

Robert Havell's 1835 engraving of Audubon's *Eider Ducks* hangs over the setting's eighteenth-century English oak dresser.

On the dresser a majestically scaled cobalt glazed Italian ceramic carp of Japanese inspiration holds a bright red Christmas apple, symbolizing good luck, longevity, and happiness.

The setting is backed by a duck hunting blind, cattails and rushes gathered from the bayou.

Mrs. Russell Long

Supper After the Opera

In 1754 or '55, Louis XV's Royal Porcelain Manufactory at Vincennes created a new, rich, pale green color for Mme. de Pompadour, Louis's "Protectrice of the Arts" and the inspired directress and propagandist of Vincennes.

Today, Mrs. Ezra Zilkha, frequent chairman of the Metropolitan Opera's Opening Night Gala Committee and one of America's leading protectrices and propagandists of the arts, uses "le vert Louis Quinze" to set the discreetly luxurious tone of a holiday season supper after the opera. The subtlety of coloring brings depth and nuance to the evening's décor.

Mrs. Zilkha's round table is skirted with gold mesh and set with Tiffany's "English King" flat silver, gadrooned service plates and "Green Cardinale" handpainted Private Stock bone china.

The pale green double bows atop the presents at each place further the setting's color scheme and echo the passementerie pattern of the china.

The centerpiece, a tall Venetian glass footed cup filled with red-and-green lady apples, holds an umbrella of orchids and ivy.

Atop the Louis XV commode sideboard, a Venetian glass dolphin compote of regal proportions holds a towering "croquembouche," the traditional holiday dessert of France.

The compote was made for Tiffany & Co. by Murano's great master glass craftsman, Archimede Seguso.

The architecture of the "croquembouche," that mechanical marvel of cuisine, was made by attaching cream puffs filled with a mixture of whipped cream and "crème pâtissière" with a "mortar" of hot caramelized sugar.

An eighteenth-century polychromed leather chinoiserie panel lends background color.

Mrs. Ezra Zilkha

80 Cities, 80 Days

Somewhere in every one of us there's a bit of Peter Pan and Nellie Forbush, of Annie Oakley and Maria von Trapp; and there's a Rolls-Royce waiting, an oasis in the noisy crowd, to take us from stage to stage.

The "21" Club will see to it that there are roast beef sandwiches and cold roast chicken in the dressing room after matinées, and champagne in the back of the Rolls on tour between one-night stands. Tiffany & Co. will provide us with jewels, silver, crystal, and porcelains to serve our daily needs.

There will be the welcome songs sung by that most American of muses, Mary Martin, who knows the world of illusion from A for Annie to Z for Ziegfeld.

There will be a flower or two from an admirer or two.

A spirited voice like Mary Martin's will cheer us on, jauntily shouting, "I Won't Grow Up," and why should I? "My Cup Runneth Over."

Mary Martin

Acknowledgments

Tiffany & Co. wishes to thank Pan American World Airways for their collaboration on *Tiffany Taste* and for seeing that all our destinations were reached in style and comfort; Mrs. Robert ("Katie") Kean for her ideas and enthusiasm; Mr. John Fling of Tiffany's Design Department for his initial layout of *Tiffany Taste;* Miss Catherine Flynn for her collaboration on recipes and food styling; Miss Nancy Holmes for her coordination and supervision of travel; Mr. Pierre Lahaussois for his overall assistance in every phase of the production of *Tiffany Taste;* and Mr. John Funt for his role in the styling and preparation of New York locations.

"Clippers and Caviar": Pan Am 747: Pan American World Airways. "All Laborde": furniture and food: The Laborde House Hotel, Rio Grande City, Texas. "The House Befitting Heaven": The Presidential Suite and food: The Halekulani Hotel, Waikiki Beach, Honolulu, Hawaii. "Iolani Palace Dinner": use of the Iolani Palace Dining Room and all furniture and props: Mr. Henry J. Bartels, curator, Iolani Palace, Honolulu, Hawaii. "Sea Lion Lunch, Regent Supper": furniture and food: The Regent Hotel, Kowloon, Hong Kong. "Lunch in the New Territories": Sculpture: Charlotte Horstman & Gerald Godfrey, Inc., Ocean Terminal, Kowloon, Hong Kong. "Kathmandu Days": furniture: Kathmandu Village Hotels, Ltd., Kathmandu, Nepal. "Tiger Tops Tables": furniture and elephants: Tiger Tops Jungle Lodge, Royal Chitwan National Park, Nepal. "Lunch in the Rana Palace Garden": furniture: The Yak and Yeti Hotel, Kathmandu, Nepal. "Royal Visit to Kronberg": interiors and furniture: Schlosshotel Kronberg, Kronberg in Taunus, Germany. "A Modest Proposal for Dinner": interior and furnishings: courtesy of The Very Reverend Victor Griffin, The Deanery, St. Patrick's Cathedral, Dublin, Ireland. "The Island of Staten": table, Newel Art Galleries, Inc.; furniture and linens, The Wicker Garden; tennis equipment and sweater, Cutler-Owens. "A Vermeil, Vermeil Special Brunch": chinoiserie blanket chest and screen: Newel Art Galleries, Inc.; kilim carpet: Doris Leslie Blau Gallery, Inc. "Luncheon at Chanel, Inc.": furniture: The Jay Spectre Collection; Chinese carpet: Doris Leslie Blau Gallery, Inc. "Verveine": furniture: Juan Portela Antiques; screen, bookcase, urn: John Roselli. "Breakfast with the Doge": antique furnishings: Olivieri. "L'Or de l'Orangerie": interior, furniture and food: Le Cirque Restaurant, New York; gilt palm tree: Newel Art Galleries, Inc. "Souper Après le Bal Masqué: interior, furnishings, food: La Grenouille Restaurant, New York. "Dinner for One, Champagne for Two": Suë et Mare Table: Didier Aaron, Inc.; Bessarabian carpet: Coury Rugs, Inc.; all other furnishings: Mara Palmer Interiors; food: The Box Tree Restaurant, New York. "Holiday Fantasy Breakfast": table and chair: Dalva Brothers, Inc.; silver bust: À La Vieille Russie; lace: Anichini Gallery; linens: Lygia Mattos. "Christmas Eve Dinner on Eaton Square": Chippendale girandoles, Regency cabinet, side chairs: Florian Papp, Inc.; dining chairs: Kentshire Galleries, Ltd. "Supper After the Opera": commode and armchairs; Didier Aaron, Inc.; chinoiserie panel: Joseph Rondina Antiques; table linens: David Forster & Co.; flowers: Philip Baloun Designs. "A Louisiana Christmas on the Bayou": oak dresser: Kentshire Galleries, Ltd.; table: Howard Kaplan's French Country Store; chairs: Hyde Park Antiques, Ltd.; Audubon engraving: Kennedy Galleries, Inc., New York. "80 Cities, 80 Days": Silver Shadow: Rolls-Royce Motors, Inc.

Photography Credits

BILLY CUNNINGHAM
Front Cover
Pages: 2–3, 8–13, 81, 85–87, 91–98, 100–1, 103–11, 113, 115–18, 122–25, 128–29, 131, 133, 136–37, 145, 147, 149, 151, 157–58, 160–61, 171–72, 174–75, 177, 179, 185, 187, 189, 191, 193, 195–96, 199, 201, 203, 205, 207–8, 211, 213, 219, 221–23.

PETER VITALE
Pages: 4–7, 11, 14, 21, 24, 27, 29, 31, 33–35, 37, 39–40, 43, 45–47, 49–53, 58, 65, 67–72, 75–76, 79, 139–40, 143, 153, 155, 163, 165–68, 181–82, 215, 217.